THE
STATE
COINAGE
OF
CONNECTICUT

by

HENRY C. MILLER

INCLUDING A MAJOR NEW SUPPLEMENT
OF PHOTOGRAPHIC PLATES AND DATA
OF VIRTUALLY ALL KNOWN VARIETIES
OF CONNECTICUT CENTS

SANFORD J. DURST
NUMISMATIC PUBLICATIONS
NEW YORK, NY

LC No 81-67127
ISBN No 0-915262-64-9

Sanford J. Durst
170 East 61st Street
New York, NY 10021

Originally published by the
American Numismatic Society
in 1920
and reprinted with their kind permission.

A significant new supplement has been added to this classic volume on the early Colonial Coinage of the State of Connecticut. It consists of 30 pages of outstanding new photographic plates (the 5 original plates are included but are admittedly not of fine quality). The illustrations on the new plates are of over 300, nearly all, of the known Miller varieties of Connecticut Cents. They appeared in the now famous Pine Tree Auction of February 15, 1975, and with other related written matter, are reprinted here with the very kind permission of Dr. Stanley Apfelbaum, President of First Coinvestors, Inc., of Albertson, N.Y., the parent corporation of Pine Tree Auction Company, Inc.

This book has been produced with an attractive, quality, durable cover. It is the opinion of the publisher that paper dust jackets are ecologically wasteful, and for that reason are not provided.

CONTENTS

THE
STATE COINAGE OF CONNECTICUT
DESCRIPTIVE LIST OF VARIETIES
By HENRY C. MILLER

Collectors of American Colonial coins have found considerable difficulty in arranging the copper issues of the State of Connecticut for the years 1785 to 1788. Mr. Crosby's "Early Coins of America," published in 1875, contains a partial list of types, and Dr. Hall in 1892 furnished a description of the then known varieties and combinations of the year 1787. Their work, excellent as far as it goes, only partly covers the ground. Some corrections and changes are called for and new material has resulted from later researches.

At the request of many collectors it has been decided to publish the present revised catalogue of varieties. The object is twofold: first, to furnish a detailed description, as nearly complete as possible, of all known dies and their combinations; second, to simplify and systematize the arrangement so that any specimen may be readily placed. Wherever available free use has been made of the data given by Crosby, Hall and Hays, and valuable assistance has been rendered by other numismatists. Especial acknowledgments are due to Messrs. Frederick A. Canfield of Dover, N. J., Hillyer Ryder of Carmel, N. Y., David Proskey of New York City, and Dr. Geo. R. Ross of Lebanon, Pa.; also to Howland Wood of the American Numismatic Society for important aid in preparing the list for publication.

In the year 1739 a petition was presented by John Read of Boston to the Governor and General Court at New Haven, asking aid in procuring a patent from the Crown to coin copper for circulation in Connecticut. It is conjectured that this application had some connection with the operations of John Higley of Granby, who, without official authority, for several years had been coining copper three-pence on his own account. No action appears to have been taken in regard to this petition and for nearly half a century the currency of Connecticut consisted almost entirely of depreciated paper with a scanty supply of English half-pence.

By act of the General Assembly of Connecticut in October, 1785, authority was granted to Samuel Bishop, Joseph Hopkins, James Hillhouse and John Goodrich to establish a mint for the manufacture of copper coins. The dies were made by Abel Buel of New Haven, but unauthorized issues of light weight and inferior workmanship circulated freely together with the legalized coins. The historic details in regard to the Connecticut coinage are given at length in Crosby's " Early Coins of America."

One general design was employed for the entire four years.

Obverse — Laureated head with bust either mailed or draped.
       Legend — AUCTORI   CONNEC
Reverse — The goddess of Liberty, seated, facing left, an olive branch in her right hand, staff surmounted by liberty cap in her left.
       Legend — INDE   ET LIB
       Date in exergue. Borders milled or serrated. Edges plain.

The coins of Connecticut vary greatly in weight. Specimens are found weighing not more than 108 grains, while others range from 168 to 184 grains. In some cases the lighter coins are probably counterfeits of the time, but many of light weight, undoubtedly authentic, are from the same dies as the heavier ones. In fact the weight and character of the planchet seems to have been regarded of little importance.

Overstrikes are frequent, resulting sometimes in a curious mixing of legends. For this purpose the Nova Constellatio and New Jersey issues appear to have been especially favored.

Owing to the scarcity of Coppers in the Colonial period from 1783 to the establishment of the United States mint, the country was flooded with a quantity of counterfeit and light weight British half-pence. Some of these were sent from abroad, but the close resemblance of others to the Connecticut coins is fairly conclusive evidence that many of these half-pence were struck in that State. As the legends on these pieces bear no reference to Connecticut they are not included in this list. On the other hand no attempt has been made to decide on the legality of any of the coins with the legend AUCTORI CONNEC. They were all made at the same epoch, some by fairly competent hands, others evidently by novices in die-sinking.

According to our list the number of dies is as follows: Obverse 199, Reverse 186. Of 1785 there 21 obverse and 20 reverse dies; of 1786, 21 obverse and 20 reverse ; 1787 affords the greatest number, 129 obverses and 124 reverses, while 1788 gives us only 28 obverses and 20 reverses. In this enumeration Crosby's obverses 23 and 35 are not included. No authentic specimens of these numbers have been located, and it is altogether probable that his descriptions of them were made from worn or imperfect pieces of other types. As the evidence against them is of course purely negative, these numbers have been retained for the present in the type-tables, but excluded from the list of combinations.

On account of the marked differences in punctuation and in the ornamental devices on many of the dies, together with the curious blunders in the spelling of the legends, this series affords a fertile and most interesting field for the collector of varieties.

It has seemed best, as far as possible, to retain the obverse types of Crosby and Hall, but a simpler method of denoting the reverses has been adopted. Obverse varieties of types 33 and 37 of 1787 evidently were numbered by Dr. Hall mostly in the order in which he found them. As these varieties are numerous it requires more patience than most collectors possess to locate a specimen according to Hall's list. It is believed that the more systematic method here employed will render the task much easier.

The question of rarity is one that admits of some difference of opinion. The degrees given by Crosby in many cases require modification. From the personal examination of many thousands of coins and the conclusions of active collectors it may be assumed that the estimates here given are approximately correct. Varieties marked C, R^1 and R^2 may generally be procured in good condition; those of R^3, R^4 and R^5 are much harder to find, while specimens of R^6, even when poor, are seldom obtainable. In fact a number of the varieties of R^6 are described from a single piece, the only one known. So many of the Connecticuts were weakly and imperfectly struck that really fine, well-centered pieces of all but a very few of the types are decidedly rare.

While the table of combinations is the most comprehensive one yet published it is, of course, possible that from time to time a few additional mulings may be found. Such pieces may safely be considered of the highest rarity.

For the convenience of those familiar with Dr. Hall's descriptions his corresponding numbers of 1787 are given in parallel columns.

TABLE OF TYPES

1785 — OBVERSE

Type	Head Facing	Legend and Punctuation		No. of Dies	With Reverse
1	Right	AUCTORI.	CONNEC.	1	E
2	"	AUCTORI : (Lower dot of 1st colon clear of head)	CONNEC :	2	A
3	"	AUCTORI : (Lower dot of colon close on head)	CONNEC :	5	A, B, F, L
4	"	AUCTORI : (Lower dot of colon partly on head)	CONNEC :	4	A C, D, F
5	"	AUCTORI : (Lower dot of colon half on head)	CONNEC :	2	F
6	"	AUCTORI : (Colon and I part on head)	CONNEC :	5	A, F, G, I, K, M
7	Left	AUCTORI	CONNEC	1	D
8	"	AUCTORI :	CONNEC :	1	D

1786 — OBVERSE

Type	Head Facing	Bust	Legend and Punctuation		No. of Dies	With Reverse
1	Right	Mailed	AUCTORI	CONNEC	1	A
2	"	"	AUCTORI •	CONNEC •	2	A, D
3	"	"	AUCTORI :	CONNEC :	1	D
4	Left	"	AUCTORI	CONNEC	2	G, R
5	"	"	AUCTORI :	CONNEC :	12	B, C, F, G, H, I, L, M, N, O, P, Q, R
6	"	Draped	AUCTORI :	CONNEC :	1	K
7	"	"	AUCTORI : ✿	✿ CONNEC : ✿	1	K
8	"	Mailed	UCTORI :	CONNNEC :	1	O

1785 — Reverse

Type	Legend and Punctuation		No. of Dies	With Obverse
A	INDE :	ETLIB :	4	2, 3, 4, 6
B	INDE : ✛	ETLIB :	1	3
C	INDE : ⁖ ⁖	ETLIB :	1	4
D	INDE : •⦂•	ETLIB :	1	4, 7, 8
E	INDE . ⁖ ⁖	ETLIB . •⦂•	1	1
F	INDE : ⊕	ETLIB :	5	3, 4, 5, 6
G	INDE : ⊕ ⊕	ET LIB :	2	6
H	INDE : ⦂	ET • LIB :	3	4, 5
I	INDE : ⦂	ETLIB :	1	6
K	INDE : ⦂	ETLIB :	2	3, 6
L	INDE : ⌗	ETLIB :	1	3
M	INDE : ⊕	ET LIB ⊕	1	6

1786 — Reverse

Type	Legend and Punctuation		No. of Dies	With Obverse
A	ET LIB	INDE	1	1, 2
B	INDE	ET LIB	2	5
C	INDE	ET LIB :	1	5 (?)
D	INDE .	ET LIB .	4	2, 3
E	INDE : ⦂	ET LIB :	1	5 (?)
F	INDE . -⦂-	ET LIB :	1	5
G	INDE : -⦂-	ET • LIB :	1	4, 5
H	INDE :	ET • LIB :	2	5
I	INDE : ⦂	ET • LIB :	1	5
K	-⦂- INDE : -⦂-	-⦂- ET - LIB :	1	6, 7
L	INDE : ⩊	ET - LIB :	1	5.
M	INDE ⫽	ET LIB	1	5
N	INDE : -⦂-	ET • LIB :	1	5
O	INDE : - ⦂ -	ET LIB :	2	5
P	INDE :	ET - LIB :	1	5
Q	INDE : -◄	ET - LIB :	1	5
R	INDE : ⦂	ET - LIB :	1	4, 5

1787 — OBVERSE

Type	Head Facing	Bust	Legend and Punctuation		No. of Dies	With Reverse
1	Right	Mailed	AUCTORI	CONNEC	4	A, C, L, VV, WW
2	Left	"	AUCTORI	CONNEC	1	B
3	"	"	AUCTORI	CONNEC •	1	G
4	"	"	AUCTORI •	CONNEC •	1	L
5	"	"	• AUCTORI •	• CONNEC	1	P
6	"	"	• AUCTORI •	• CONNEC •	2	M
7	"	"	AUCTORI :	CONNEC :	1	I
8	"	"	AUCTORI : ∴	∴ CONNEC : •∴•	1	N, O
9	"	"	× AUCTORI +	× × CONNEC ×	1	D, E, R
10	"	"	+ AUCTORI × ×	+ + CONNEC +	1	E
11	"	"	✱ AUCTORI ✱	✱ CONNEC ✱	3	E, K
12	"	"	AUCTORI. ✿	CONNEC ✿	1	Q
13	"	"	AUCTORI ✱	✱ CONNEC ✱	1	D
14	"	"	→ AUCTORI ←	→ → CONNEC. ←	1	H
15	"	"	✿ AUCTORI ✿ ✿	✿ ✿ CONNECT ✿ ✿	1	F, R, S
16	"	Draped.	AUCTORI :	CONNEC :	6	l, m, n, p, u, NN
17	"	"	AUCTORI :	- ✚ -CONNEC :	1	g
18	"	"	AUCTORI : ✚	✚ CONNEC	1	g
19	"	"	AUCTORI : ✚	✚ CONNEC :	1	g
20	"	"	AUCTORI : ✱	✱ CONNEC :	1	a
21	"	"	AUCTORI : ×	- ✚ - CONNEC : ×	1	DD
22	"	"	AUCTORI : ✱	✚ CONNEC : ×	1	g
23	"	"	AUCTORI : ✚-	- ✚ - CONNEC : -✚-	?	?
24	"	"	- ✚ - AUCTORI :	- ✚ - CONNEC :	1	g, FF
25	"	"	✱ AUCTORI : ×	✱ CONNEC :	1	b, m
26	"	"	✱ AUCTORI :	× CONNEC : ×	1	a, kk, AA
27	"	"	✚ AUCTORI : ×	× CONNEC : ×	1	a
28	"	"	AUCTORI : ✱	✱ CONNEC :	1	m, n, o
29	"	"	AUCTORI : ✱	✱ CONNEC : ✱	2	N, n, o, p, aa
30	"	"	AUCTORI : ✿	✿ CONNEC : ✿	1	X, hh
31	"	"	✿ AUCTORI : ✿	✿ CONNEC :	2	r, gg
32	"	"	✿ AUCTORI . ✿	✿ CONNEC . ✿	8	X, Z, aa
33	"	"	✿ AUCTORI : ✿	✿ CONNEC : ✿	45	{ T, W, Z, l, q, r, s, ff, gg, hh, II, KK, SS
34	"	"	AUCTORI : ←	→ CONNEC : ←	2	k, ff
35	"	"	AUCTORI : ←	→ CONNEC : ←	?	
36	"	"	→ AUCTORI : ←	→ CONNEC :	1	k, l, ff
37	"	"	→ AUCTORI : ←	→ CONNEC : ←	14	{ B, e, h, i, k, cc, ff, HH, LL, RR, TT
38	"	"	AUCIORI :	✚ CONNEC : ×	1	l, gg
39	"	"	→ AUCTOBI : ←	→ CONNEC : ←	2	h, ee, ff
40	"	"	AUCTOPI ✱	✱ CONNEC	1	N, kk
41	"	"	✱ AUCTOPI : ✱	✱ CONNEC :	1	ii
42	"	"	✱ AUCTOPI :	✱ CONNEC . ✱	1	o, kk
43	"	"	✿ AUCTORI . ✿	✿ CONNFC . ✿	1	Y
44	"	"	✿ AUCTORI :	✿ CONNEC : ✿	1	W, Z
45	"	"	-×- AUCTORI : -✚-	-×- CONNEC : -✚-	1	CC
46	"	"	✱ AUCTORI : ×-	-×- CONNEC : -×-	1	BB
47	"	"	✿ AUCTORI : -×-	-×- CONNEC :	1	a
48	"	"	→ AUCTORI : ←•	•••→ CONNEC : ←	1	g
49	"	"	✿ AUCTORI : ✿	✿ ✿ CONNEC : ✿	1	Z

1787 — REVERSE

Type	Legend and Punctuation		No. of Dies	With Obverse
A	ETLIB	INDE	1	1
B	INDE ET	LIB	1	2, 37
C	INDE · ET	LIB	1	1
D	+ INDE + ET + + +	+ LIB + +	1	9, 13
E	* INDE * ET *	* LIB * *	1	9, 10, 11
F	✿ INDE ✿ ET ✿ ✿ ✿	✿ LIB ✿ ✿	1	15, 50, 55
G	INDE * ET	LIB *	1	8, 52
H	INDE · ET ⇉	⇉ LIB. ⇇	1	14
I	INDE : ∴	ET LIB.	1	7
K	* INDE *	* ET LIB *	1	11
L	INDE ·	ET · LIB ·	1	1, 4
M	INDE : * *	* ET · LIB :	1	6
N	INDE * *	* ETLIB *	1	8, 29, 40
O	* INDE : * *	* ETLIB : *	1	8
P	· IN DE ·	ET LIB ·	1	5
Q	✿ IN DE ·	ETLIB · ✿	1	12
R	+ IND × × + ET +	× + + LIB + + ×	1	9, 15
S	✿ INDL ✿ ET ✿	✿ LIB ✿	1	15
T	✿ INDE : ✿ ✿	✿ ETLIB : ✿	2	33
V	✿ INDE . ✿ ✿ ✿	✿ ET LIB ·	?	?
W	✿ INDE : ✿ ✿ ✿	✿ ETLIB :	6	33, 44
X	✿ INDE . ✿ ✿ ✿	✿ ETLIB . ✿	6	30, 32
Y	✿ INDE . ✿ — ✿ — ✿	✿ ETLIB . ✿	1	48
Z	✿ INDE : ✿ ✿ ✿	✿ ETLIB : ✿	24	33, 44, 49
a	× INDE : — + — — + —	— + — ETLIB :	3	20, 26, 27, 29, 47
b	× INDE : — + — — + —	+ — ETLIB :	1	25
c	+ — INDE : — + — — + —	— + — ETLIB :	?	?
d	* INDE : +	+ ETLIB :	?	?
e	+ INDE : ⇇⇇	+ ETLIB :	1	37
f	— + — INDE : + +	— + — ET — LIB :	?	?
g	— + — INDE : — + — — + —	— + — ET — LIB :	5	17, 18, 19, 22, 24, 48
h	+ INDE : ⇇⇇	× ET — LIB :	2	37, 39
i	+ INDE : ⇇⇇	· ⁄⁄ ET — LIB : ×	1	37
k	⁄⁄ INDE : ⇇⇇	⁄⁄ ET — LIB :	5	34, 36, 37
l	⇇⇇ INDE : ⇇⇇	⇇⇇ ET — LIB : ⇇	2	16, 33, 36, 38
m	* INDE * *	* ET — LIB *	1	16, 25, 28
n	* INDE : * *	* ET — LIB :	1	16, 28, 29
o	* INDE * *	ETLIB *	1	28, 29, 42
p	* INDE * *	* ETLIB *	1	16, 29
q	INDE : ✿ ✿ *	✿ ETLIB : ✿	1	33
r	✿ INDE : ✿ ✿	✿ ET LIB :	5	31, 33
s	✿ INDE : ✿ ✿	✿ ET — LIB : ✿	2	33
u	✿ INDE ✿ ✿	✿ ETLIB	1	16
aa	✿ FNDE . ✿ ✿ ✿	✿ ETLIB . ✿	1	32
bb	× INDE : — + — — + —	— + — ETLIR :	?	?
cc	⁄⁄ INDE : ⇇⇇	⁄⁄ ET — LIR :	2	37
dd	⇉⇇ INDE : ⇇⇇	⇇ ET — LIR : ⇇	?	?
ee	⇉⇇ INDE : ⇇⇇	⇉⇇ ET — LIR :	1	39
ff	⇇⇇ INDE : ⇇⇇	⇇⇇ ET — LIR : ⇇	2	33, 34, 36, 37, 39
gg	✿ INDE : ✿ ✿	✿ ETLIR : ✿	2	31, 33
hh	✿ INDE : ✿ ✿ ✿	✿ ETLIR : ✿	2	30, 33

1787 — OBVERSE

Type	Head Facing	Bust	Legend and Punctuation		No. of Dies	With Reverse
50	Left	Draped	✿ AUCTORI . ✿	✿ CONNLC . ✿	1	F
51	"	"	Same as 29²			
52	Right	Mailed	AUCTORI	CONNEC .	1	G
53	Left	Draped	➜ AUCTORI : ✦	•➜ CONNEC : ✦	1	FF
54	"	"	Same as 21			
55	"	Mailed	✿ AUCTORI . ✿	✿ CONNEC . ✿	1	F

1788 — OBVERSE

Type	Legend and Punctuation		No. of Dies	With Reverse
1	AUCTORI	CONNEC	1	I
2	✱ AUCTORI •	CONNEC ✐	1	D
3	♣ AUCTORI ✱	✱ CONNEC ✱	2	B
4	AUCTORI ✱	✱ CONNEC ✦	2	B, K, R
5	✱ AUCTORI ✱	• CONNEC ✦	1	B
6	AUCTORI ✱	✱ CONNEC ✱	1	H
7	✱ AUCTORI ✱	✦ CONNEC ✱	1	E, F, K
8	AUCTORI. ✿	CONNEC ✿	1	K
9	AUCTORI	CONNEC ✱	1	E
10	AUCTORI ✱	✱ CONNEC ✱	1	C
11	✱ AUCTORI	✱ CONNEC ✱	1	G
12	✱ AUCTORI ✱	✱ CONNEC ✱	2	C, E
13	✿ AUCTORI ✿	✿ CONNLC ✿	1	A
14	✿ AUCTORI ✿	✿ CONNEC ✿	2	A, L
15	✿ AUCTORI ✿	✿ CONNEC. ✐	2	L, P
16	✿ AUCTORI. ✿	✿ CONNEC. ✿	6	D, H, L, N, O
17	✿ AUCTORI. ✿	✿ CONNLC. ✿	1	O, Q

1787 — REVERSE

Type	Legend and Punctuation		No. of Dies	With Obverse
ii	✿ INDE :✿ ✿	✿ ETIIB :	1	41
kk	✿ INDE :✿	✿ ETIIB : ✿	2	26, 40, 42
AA	✿ INDE :+ − +	+ ETLIB :	1	26
BB	✕ INDE :+ −+−	+ ETLIB •	1	46
CC	+ INDE : −✳− ✳−	−+− ET LIB :	1	45
DD	−+−INDE : + −+−	−+− ET-LIB :	1	21
EE	✿ INDE : ✿−✿−	− ✿ ET-LIB : ✿	1	33
FF	−+−INDE : + +	+ ET-LIB :	1	24, 53
GG	−+−INDE : −+=+−	−+− ET-LIB :	1	38
HH	➤← INDE : ←←•	← ET-LIB : ←	1	37
II	✿ INDE : ✿ ✿ ✿	✿ ETLIB ✿	1	33
KK	✿ INDE : ✿ ✿ ✿	ET LIB : ✿	1	33
LL	✿ INDE : ✿ ✿	✿ ET • I IB : ✿	1	37
NN	✿ INDE : ✿ ✿	✿ ET • LIB :	2	16
RR	➤← INDE : ←←•	➤← ET-LIB : ←	1	37
SS	✿ INDE : ✿ •✿•	− ✿ ET • LIB : ✿	1	33
TT	− ✿ −INDE : ✿ ✿	− ✿ − ETLIB : ✿	1	37
VV	INDE	ETLIB •	1	1
WW	ET LIB	INDE •	1	1

1788 — REVERSE

Type	Legend and Punctuation		No. of Dies	With Obverse
A	✿ INDE ✿ ET ✿	✿ ✿ LIB ✿	2	13, 14
B	INDE ✿ ET	LIB ✿	2	3, 4, 5
C	INDE ✿ ET	LIB ✿	1	10, 12
D	INDE. ✿ ET ✿	LIB ✿	1	2, 16
E	INDE ✿ ET ✿	✿ LIB ✿	1	7, 9, 12
F	INDE ✿ ET ✿	✿ LIB ✿	1	7, 12
G	INDE ✿ ET ✿	✿ LIB ✿	1	11
H	INDE. ✿ ✿	✿ ETLIB. ✿	1	6, 16
I	INDE ✕	ET • LIB ✕	1	1
K	✿ INDE ✿	ET ✿ LIB ✿	1	4, 7, 8
L	✿ INDE • ET ✿	✿ LIB. ✿	2	14, 15, 16
M	INDE • ET ✿	✿ LIB. ✿	?	?
N	✿ IN DE. ✿ ✿	✿ ✿ ETLIB. ✿	1	16
O	✿ INDL. ET ✿ ✿	✿ ✿ LIB. ✿	1	16, 17
P	✿ INDE • ET ✿ ✿	✿ ✿ LIB. ✿	1	15
Q	✿ INDE • ET ✿	✿ ✿ LIB. ✿	1	17
R	✕ INDE ✿ ✿ ET	✿ LIB ✿	1	4

DESCRIPTIVE LIST OF VARIETIES

1785 OBVERSE

Types 1 to 6 have mailed bust facing right.

Obverse 1.

AUCTORI.   CONNEC.

Fillet-ends long, ending between the bust and the legend.   1—E (R^4)

Obverse 2.

AUCTORI :   CONNEC :

Lower dot of colon clear of head. Both fillet-ends point at A.

             2—A^1 (R^3). 2—A^4 (R^3)

Obverse 3.

AUCTORI :   CONNEC :

Lower dot of colon very close to or touching head.

Var. 1. A single sprig from near top of front leaf turns back over forehead. Depression over cheek. Upper curved line of mail ends abruptly at lower left corner and does not connect with inner line. Five dots below upper curved line. Four dots on mail above breast. 3^1—A^3 (R^3). 3^1—L

Var. 2. A single sprig from near top of upper front leaf is joined by a second, both terminating in a prominent berry on forehead. T slopes to right, its top above adjoining C. I low. The curved lines of the mail at lower left corner form a rounded extremity. Lower curved line double. 3^2—L (R^3)

Var. 3. Two sprigs from top leaf arch over forehead. Colons heavy. Last colon close to C and low. 3^3—F^3 (R^4)

Var. 4. A single sprig from top leaf branches over forehead, arching backward, the upper termination heavy and connecting with top of front leaf. Both colons low, the dots smaller than in var. 3. At lower left corner the mail ends in a sharp point.

            3^4—F^1 (R^3). 3^4—F^2 (R^3)

Var. 5. Four hair locks emerge from upper front leaf, uniting over forehead. Top of T above that of C. A line joins T and O at top. Letters of CONNEC irregular with EC low 3^5—B (R^2)

Obverse 4.

AUCTORI :   CONNEC :

Lower dot of colon partly on head.

Var. 1. Head and legend very large. Lower fillet-end near A. AU widely spaced. Last colon much nearer to C than to mail. Hair brushed downward. The usual variety of the Negro Head. 4^1—F^4 (R^1)

Var. 2. Similar to var. 1, but hair brushed back. Lower dot of last colon heavy. The rare variety of the Negro Head. 4^2—F^4 (R^6)

Of this variety only one authentic specimen is known.

Var. 3. Lower fillet-end distant from A. AUCTORI closely spaced. Hair brushed back, forehead receding. Last colon midway between C and mail. Break from lower left corner of mail. 4^3—A^2 (R^3). 4^3—D (R^4)

Var. 4. Four hair locks from upper front leaf unite in a prominent berry over forehead. Mail at lower left corner has rounded extremity. Long pointed nose, lips thick. Upper fillet points between A and U. EC low. 4^4—C (R^4). 4^4—D (R^4)

Obverse 5.

AUCTORI :   CONNEC :

Lower dot of colon half on head.

Var. 1. Lower fillet-end distant from A, upper one rather close to U. AUC closely spaced. Lower dot of last colon slightly below line of C. C in CONNEC closed. Neck large and badly shaped. Two oblong die-breaks between chin and bust.
5^1—F^5 (R^4)

Var. 2. AUC more widely spaced than in var. 1. Upper fillet-end further from U. Lower dot of last colon below line of C. Colons further from I and C than in var. 1. Period-like dot in field between upper part of mail and last colon. 5^2—F^5 (R^4)

Obverse 6.

AUCTORI :   CONNEC :

Lower dot of colon entirely on head. I partly on head.

Var. 1. Prominent berry on forehead. Tail of R close to I and touches head. Last colon distant from mail and much nearer C. 6^1—A^1 (R^3)

Var. 2. Tail of R touches I but is clear of head. Last colon close to C and low. Breaks near milling before CONNEC, on head in front of wreath, and from forehead through face and field to corner of mail. 6^2—F^1 (R^4)

Var. 3. Fillet-ends between bust and A. A touches upper fillet. Hair very coarse. C distant from forelock. 6^3—G^1 (R^3). 6^3—G^2 (R^4)

Var. 4. Lower fillet-end distant from A. Lower left corner of mail ends in sharp point. T in AUCTORI high. Last colon nearly equi-distant from C and mail. Die-break at foot of A, in late impressions connecting A with mail.
6^4—F^5 (R^5). 6^4—I (R^3). 6^4—K^1 (R^5)

Var. 5. Fillet-ends between bust and A. Letters light and tall. I low and prolonged below the bottom of R. Last colon more distant from the bust than in var. 3. Die-break over NNE. 6^5—M (R^5)

Obverse 7.

AUCTORI   CONNEC

Mailed bust facing left. Head of '86. Milling fine, but most of it lacking. Some specimens show a heavy die-break from neck through lower end of the fillets.
7—D (R^5)

Obverse 8.

AUCTORI :   CONNEC :

Mailed bust facing left. Similar to type 7 but with the addition of colons to the legend. Large letters. Oblong break in field in front of nose. One of the rarest types of 1785. Crosby found only one. 8—D (R^6)

1785 REVERSE

Reverse A

INDE :   ETLIB :

Goddess of Liberty seated, facing left, olive branch in right hand, liberty pole with cap in left.

Var. 1.   Branch-hand points at D and space between D and E.   Branch very close to inner dot of colon, its top about on a level with upper part of colon.   B a trifle low. Last colon also low, the lower dot nearer B.   2—A^1.   6—A^1

Var. 2.   Branch-hand points at E and space between E and colon.   Inner dot partly on branch which extends considerably above colon.   Last colon not far from date-line.   In date 1 broad and high.   4^3—A^2

Var. 3.   Branch-hand points at first colon.   Branch curved.   The folds of the skirt very prominent.   E in INDE low and out of position.   Lower dot of colon close to stem of branch.   3^1—A^3

Var. 4.   Branch-hand points at D and space between D and E.   Top of upper leaf considerably above colon.   A second scroll projects downward from shield directly over the figure 5.   2—A^4

Reverse B.

INDE : ⁘   ETLIB :

Branch-hand opposite E.   Cross formed by four irregular heavy dots with light connecting line.   Top of branch close to cross.   Lower dot of first colon close to leaves on left.   Base of E's defective.   Compare Rev. K and Rev. L.   3^5—B

Reverse C.

INDE : ∴ ∴   ETLIB :

The second group of 4 dots irregular.   Leaves of branch close.   Date wide.

4^4—C

Reverse D.

INDE : •:•   ETLIB :

Branch-hand opposite colon.   Stem of branch thin and weak.   Five leaves on left, four on right.   4^3—D.   4^4—D.   7—D.   8—D

Reverse E.

INDE. •:• •:•   ET LIB . •:•

Periods large and heavy.   Figures of date small.   Top of 5 touches date line.

1—E

Reverse F.

INDE : ✪   ET LIB :

Var. 1.   Branch-hand points at D.   I in INDE distant from date line.   First colon low, the lower dot very close to E and merging into outer leaf of branch.   LI close at base.   Last colon close to B.   Break through top of 8, extending more than half way towards 5.   3^4—F^1.   6^2—F^1

Var. 2. Branch-hand points at first colon and space between E and colon. I in INDE distant from date line, but not so far as in var. 1. First colon low, but clear of E and branch. Lower curve of B defective. 3^4—F^2

Var. 3. Branch-hand points at first colon. I near date line. Upper date line heavy. First colon sloping and further from E than in var. 5. 3^3—F^3

Var. 4. Branch-hand points at E. Letters of legend heavy. Third leaf on left of branch touches inner dot of colon. Lower dot of last colon close to rim of shield.
4^1—F^4. 4^2—F^4.

Var. 5. Branch-hand points at first colon. Large, heavy letters. I in INDE near date line. Last colon low, rather distant from shield. Date lines uniform.
5^1—F^5. 5^2—F^5. 6^4—F^5

Reverse G

INDE : ❖ ❖   ET LIB :

Var. 1. Top of branch opposite centre of first quatrefoil. Liberty cap unusually large. Date line ends opposite foot of Liberty. 6^3—G^1

Var. 2. Top of branch about level with lowest part of first quatrefoil. Liberty cap small. 6^3—G^2

Reverse H.

INDE : ∴   ET-LIB :

Crosby gives this reverse with obverses 4 and 5.

Reverse I.

INDE : ∴   ET LIB :

Lower dot of first colon close to branch and might be taken for a leaf. Stem heavy and continuous. I slants to left. N is further from I than from D. The punctuation after first colon shows 4 regularly placed period-like dots, under which is a comma nearly united to the lowest dot. Late impressions show die-breaks from I to milling, between N and D, and between T and L. There are also cracks along the top of TL and the base of LIB. 6^4—I

Reverse K.

INDE :   ∴•   ET LIB :

In worn specimens it is not easy to distinguish the group of 4 large periods from the heavy cross in Rev. B. and Rev. L. In such cases the type must be determined from other details which show a marked difference.

Var. 1. Top of I above top of N in INDE. Foliage abundant, top leaf disconnected. Bottom of I double-cut. Branch-hand points at E and space between E and colon. Last colon near date line. 6^4—K^1

Var. 2. Top of I and N nearly on same plane. Base of both E's defective. Last colon distant from date line. Possibly a duplication of Rev. B, with the connecting lines of the cross not showing. 3^5—K^2

Reverse L.

INDE : ⠶   ET LIB :

The group following first colon is a heavy cross like Rev. B with addition of 4 irregularly shaped dots. Branch-hand points at E.

Specimens sharp enough to show the dots added to the cross are very scarce. Pieces not showing these dots might easily be classified as Rev. B. The branch, however, is quite different from B. 3^1—L. 3^2—L

Reverse M.

INDE : ⚜   ET LIB : ⚜

Branch-hand points above colon. Letters tall. First quatrefoil about twice as far from colon as from head. Upper dot of both colons low. Date line double, the upper stroke the heavier. Not in Crosby. 6^5—M

1786 OBVERSE

Obverse 1.

AUCTORI   CONNEC

Mailed bust facing right. Rudely cut die with heavy features and double chin. Ribbon bow with long, coarse ribbon-ends. Sometimes struck on light planchets.

1—A (R^4)

Obverse 2.

AUCTORI •   CONNEC •

Mailed bust facing right.

Var. 1. Head of better work than in type 1. Ribbon-ends lighter and NE more widely spaced. Eight leaves in wreath. Periods opposite centre of letters.

2^1—A (R^3). 2^1—D^3 (R^6)

Var. 2. Head large, similar to Obv. 3. Broad shoulders. Periods opposite lowest part of letters. A distant from mail. Not in Crosby. 2^2—D^2 (R^5)

Obverse 3.

AUCTORI :   CONNEC :

Mailed bust right. Head large, largest of the year. A near mail. All letters in CONNEC distant from head. 3—D^1 (R^4). 3—D^4 (R^6)

Obverse 4.

AUCTORI   CONNEC

Mailed bust left.

Var. 1. Coarse, serrated milling. Letters in CONNEC all touch milling.

4^1—G (R^2)

Var. 2. Fine milling. Heavy break from neck through fillet-ends. Same die as Obv. 7 of 1785. 4^2—R (R^5)

Obverse 5.

AUCTORI :   CONNEC :

Mailed bust left.

Var. 1. Coarse, serrated milling. The upper border of mail beneath the throat consists of a double curved line and is not fluted. The tail of the R extends too far to the right. Break through ORI. 5^1—H^1 (R^5)

Var. 2. Upper dot of both colons low. Last colon sloping, the upper dot nearer C. Four leaves on back of wreath. Three stemmed berries within wreath. Lowest curl ends in a berry which it partly includes. Fine milling. Slight break at left of o in CONNEC. 5^2—H^1 (R^5). 5^2—I (R^3). 5^2—O^2 (R^5)

Var. 3. " Hercules Head." Bust and letters deeply cut. Scowling face, neck thick, chin rectangular. I long, extending above the top of R. Same die as Obv. 7 of 1787. 5^3—B^2 (R^6). 5^3—G (R^5). 5^3—N (R^3)

Var. 4. Coarse, serrated milling. Letters NEC touch milling. Semi-spherical protrusion below the front mail. In the field above the fillets a short hyphen-like line. Upper dot of both colons low. 5^4—G (R^2). 5^4—O^1 (R^2). 5^4—N (R^6)

Var. 5. Four leaves on front, three on back of wreath. Semi-circle below mail. Edges of leaves rough and irregular. Lowest curl encircles a berry. Milling fine. First colon sloping, the lower dot nearer I. Upper dot of last colon nearly level with top of C. Break from upper fillet. 5^5—M (R^3)

Var. 6. Four leaves on back of wreath. Milling fine. Semi-circular line below mail. Both colons low, dots large and heavy. V-shaped break from last colon to border and thence to lower right point of mail. 5^6—M (R^5)

Var. 7. Upper dots of both colons about on a level with the tops of the preceding letters and somewhat farther from I and C than the lower dots. Four leaves back of wreath with rough, irregular edges. The letters NEC recut. Milling fine, in most cases partly lacking. Heavy diagonal break across neck. Semi-circular line below mail distant from milling. 5^7—H^1 (R^4). 5^7—O^2 (R^5)

Var. 8. Upper dots of both colons farthest from letters. Four leaves on back of wreath. Semi-circular line heavy, touching milling. Partial double cutting of fluted border. Break on border above and to left of CO.
                        5^8—F (R^5) 5^8—H^2 (R^5). 5^8—O^2 (R^3)

Var. 9. Upper dot of both colons low. Upper dot of first colon the nearer to I. Four leaves on back of wreath with edges smooth and not outlined. Three berries with stems in wreath. The lowest curl ends in a berry, but does not encircle it. Sharp specimens show trace of a semi-spherical elevation. No semi-circular line. Fine milling. 5^9—B^1 (R^4). 5^9—Q (R^5)

Var. 10. Upper dot of both colons low. First colon has both dots near I. Four outlined leaves back of wreath. Lowest curl ends in a berry, but does not encircle it. First C in CONNEC shows double cutting. Break closing first C in CONNEC. Another closing and extending slightly below last C. 5^{10}—L (R^4). 5^{10}—P (R^5)

Var. 11. Upper dot of both colons low, the dots much smaller than those on other dies of Obv. 5. Four leaves on back of wreath with smooth edges, not outlined. No berries. Lowest curl heavy, without berry. No semi-circular line. 5^{11}—R (R^5)

Var. 12. Differs from Var. 10 chiefly in the position of the colons. The first colon is more distant from I and the last colon closer to C than in Var. 10. In Var. 10 the first colon slants to left with both dots close to I. In Var. 12 the upper dot is considerably further than the lower one from I. The last colon is low, the lower dot mostly below C. The tail of the R is further from I than in Var. 10. 5^{12}—L (R^6)

Obverse 6.

AUCTORI :   CONNEC :

Draped bust, facing left. A distant from bust and U. U double cut, high and out of position.   Three fillet-ends.   6—K (R⁵)

Obverse 7.

AUCTORI : ✱   ✱ CONNEC : ✱

Draped bust left. A near bust. Upper fillet points at last colon.   7—K (R⁶)

Obverse 8.

UCTORI :   CONNNEC :

Mailed bust left. U near mail in the place usually occupied by A. No space left for an A. CONNNEC rather widely spaced. Chin pointed. Oblong die break back of head above the fillets.   8—O¹. Unique

This curious piece is not an overstrike. Probably the legend was so badly blundered that the die was discarded after a few trial pieces. The upper part of the reverse of the only known specimen shows the incused impression of a second obverse.

1786 REVERSE

Reverse A.

ET LIB   INDE

                                               1—A.   2¹—A

Reverse B.

INDE   ET LIB

Var. 1. Top of D slopes to right. The lowest portion of the branch stem terminates in a line deflected to right. Break from forehead left to milling; also from 7 to I in INDE. Other breaks also. The impressions of this reverse are generally weak and the planchets defective.   5⁹—B¹

Var. 2. Much stronger and better struck than Var. 1. No deflecting line from branch stem. Branch short, with seven coarse leaves. B touches shield. Die-breaks from border to back of head and through the final B. An extremely rare reverse.

                                               5³—B²

Reverse C.

INDE   ET LIB :

Crosby, 5—C. Mr. Crosby gives this combination, but no specimen of it has been located.

Reverse D.

INDE.   ET LIB.

Var. 1. Liberty cap large and very wide, touching milling. Branch points at period. Top of T in ET above top of E.   3—D¹

Var. 2.   First period distant from E.   Liberty cap large and tall, clear of milling. Branch-hand opposite D.   Top leaf points to right of period.   E in ET slants to left. Usually found on small planchets, not showing date. 2^2—D^2

2^2 D^2

Var. 3.   Legend very widely spaced.   Liberty cap large.   Branch-hand opposite N.   Branch points at lower left corner of E.   Broad, coarse milling.   Figures of date small, all close to date line, which is double. 2^1—D^3

Var. 4.   Periods in line with base of letters.   Branch-hand opposite space between N and D.   Top leaf slants to right and points to base of E.   Date line double. Figures of date all considerably below the line, except the 6 which is less distant.

3—D^4

Reverse E.

INDE : •:•   ET LIB :

Crosby gives this reverse in combination with Obv. 5.   Examples found prove on examination to be worn or weakly struck pieces generally of Rev. O.

Reverse F.

INDE. -:-   ET LIB.

The horizontal lines of the cross are larger and much heavier than the vertical lines.   Two strings below the hair-puff.   Branch-hand opposite D.   Branch short, with scanty foliage and long leaves.   Upper leaf on left points at upright of E.   No terminal leaf. 5^8—F

Reverse G.

INDE : -:-   ET • LIB :

Group of four horizontal lines near first colon.   Pole with Liberty cap.   Stem of branch short and thick, with small leaves.   Lower curve of B very close to rim of shield.   Last colon has lower dot on shield. 4^1—G. 5^3—G. 5^4—G

Reverse H.

INDE :   ET • LIB :

Var. 1.   Drapery extends well to right over shield.   Lower dot of last colon very close to shield, but not touching.   Branch wide, leaves rather long.   The stem of the branch ends in a line deflecting to right.   No Liberty cap. 5^1—H^1. 5^2—H^1. 5^7—H^1

Var. 2.   Drapery as in Var. 1.   Lower dot of last colon barely touches shield. Highest point of top leaf a trifle below the lower right corner of E.   No deflecting line from bottom of stem. 5^8—H^2

Reverse I.

INDE : • ˙• •   ET • LIB :

In the group of 4 dots between the first colon and the head the upper and lower ones are light and close, the lateral ones heavier and more distant. The elongated period between ET and LIB may have been meant for a hyphen. Lower dot of last colon entirely on shield. Branch-stem ends in a line deflecting to left. No Liberty cap. 5^2—I

Reverse K.

-˙- INDE : -˙-   -˙- ET - LIB :

The third group of 4 lines close to pole. No Liberty cap. The branch-stem is prolonged in a line slightly curved and thicker at the end.   6—K. 7—K

Reverse L.

INDE : ≑   ET - LIB :

Group of lines about midway between colon and head. Colon dots small. Last colon clear of shield. Branch short. Branch-hand opposite upright of D. Pole has Liberty cap. 5^{10}—L. 5^{12}—L
Crosby Supplement, p. 372.

Reverse M.

INDE ⁐   ET LIB

Neck long. Back of head squarely outlined by the hair. Pole has Liberty cap. From the lower left corner of the stem there is a short, curving line. Four transverse lines on globe, the upper two close.

Crosby, on page 372, refers to this reverse as B. It is, however, from a different die. 5^5—M. 5^6—M

Reverse N.

INDE : - -˙- -   ET • LIB :

The group of 6 lines is midway between first colon and head. Lower dot of first colon partly below base of E. Lower dot of last colon on shield. B touches rim of shield. Pole has cap. Date line single. 5^3—N. 5^4—N

Reverse O.

INDE : • ˙• •   ET LIB :

Var. 1. In the group of 6 dots after the first colon the upper and lowest are the largest. Leaves of branch long. Lowest leaf on left points downward, corresponding leaf on right club-shaped and points upward. Stem of branch ends in a line deflecting to left. Lower dot of last colon on shield. Liberty cap touches milling. Date line single. 5^4—O¹

Var. 2. The periods at extreme right and left of the group of 6 are both a trifle above the adjoining ones, while in Var. 1 the period at the left is a trifle low. Top of upper leaf near E. Lower dot of first colon about on line with base of E. Lowest leaf on left of branch points upward. Top leaf separated from stem. No line from bottom of stem. Lower dot of last colon on shield. No Liberty cap.

Specimens of this reverse showing distinctly the group of 6 dots are very difficult to obtain. Less perfect pieces are not especially rare. 5^2—O^2. 5^7—O^2. 5^8—O^2

Reverse P.

INDE :   ET - LIB :

This reverse differs from Rev. H in having a hyphen instead of a period between ET and LIB. Neck long. Lowest leaf on left of branch turns slightly upward. Lower dot of last colon about half on shield. Traces of double date line, the lower line heavy. Four transverse lines upon the globe about equi-distant. 5^{10}—P

Reverse Q.

INDE : - ⁕   ET-LIB :

Neck long. Stem of branch ends in a line curving to left. Four short leaves on left of branch. Terminal leaf points at lower dot of colon and is distant from it. Lower dot of last colon on shield. Three longitudinal lines on globe. Pole has Liberty cap. Double date line, the lower one heavy. The character after INDE is only approximate. Specimens found are too poor to show it exactly. 5^9—Q

5⁹   Q

Reverse R.

INDE : ⁙   ET-LIB :

Upper dot of first colon low, opposite middle of E. Branch short, with small, thick leaves. Lower dot of last colon half on shield. Fine curved line, but no drapery over shield. Date line single. 4^2—R. 5^{11}—R

1787 OBVERSE

Mailed Busts

Obverse 1.

AUCTORI   CONNEC

Mailed bust, facing right.

Var. 1. The smallest head of the year. Wreath of seven leaves. A close to mail. I close to head. C distant. Same die as Obv. 1 of 1788.
          1^1—A (R^3). 1^1—VV (R^6)

Var. 2. Largest head of the year. A close to mail, final C distant. On most specimens CONNEC weakly struck, the E not showing. " Bradford Head," " Mutton Head." 1^2—C (R^3)

Var. 3.   Medium head.   Letters large.   A six-pointed star in front at lower edge of mail.   Tip of nose opposite right edge of o.   Last c touches mail. 1^3—L (R^4)

Var. 4.   Head outlined and right of centre of planchet.   Lowest point of mail near milling.   Broken A.   c low.   Vermont c.

A die discovered by Dr. Hall after the publication of his list. 1^4—WW (R^6)

Obverse 2.

AUCTORI   CONNEC

Mailed bust, facing left.   TOR widely spaced.   Tail of R nearly touches base of I. Second N double cut.   2—B (R^3)

Obverse 3.

AUCTORI   CONNEC •

Mailed bust left.   Fillet-ends tied in a bow.   Sharp pointed A leans strongly to left.   Letters of legend irregularly spaced.   TORI on higher plane than AUC.   Final c low.   3—G (R^5)

Obverse 4.

AUCTORI •   CONNEC •

Mailed bust left.   Letters large and widely spaced.   The periods nearly opposite the centre of the letters.   Perfect die.   Found also with crescent-shape die break in front of throat.   Occasional examples with this die break are found on unusually large planchets.   On later issues the die break becomes more extended and forms a horn-like projection from the mail.

4—L.   Perfect die, R^3.   Broken die and horned bust C.   Large planchet, R^4

Obverse 5.

• AUCTORI •   • CONNEC

Mailed bust left.   Periods opposite centre of letters.   CO close.   5—P (R^6)

Obverse 6.

• AUCTORI •   • CONNEC •

Var. 1.   " Laughing Head."   Periods, except the second, opposite centre of letters.   Second period higher and nearly over top leaf of wreath.   I over hair.   Star below mail. 6^1—M (R^1)

Var. 2.   " Simple Head."   " Outlined Head."   Second period opposite centre of I and distant from wreath.   Break through star below mail to milling. 6^2—M (R^3)

Obverse 7.

AUCTORI :   CONNEC :

" Hercules Head."   CO widely spaced; also both N's.   Same die as Obv. 5 of 1786, Var. 3.   7—I (R^4)

Obverse 8.

AUCTORI : ∴   ∴ CONNEC : •∴•

In the group of four dots in front of the wreath the right horizontal dot touches the top leaf, and in poorly struck or worn specimens does not always show.   Three fillet-ends.   Break from foot of A, sometimes extending upward to the chin.

8—N (R^3).   8—O (R^3)

Obverse 9.

 × AUCTORI +   × × CONNEC ×

First crosslet low. Last crosslet near c. Berries within wreath in triplets. o in AUCTORI and co in CONNEC low.   9—D (R⁴). 9—E (R⁴). 9—R (R⁵)

Obverse 10.

+ AUCTORI × ×   · + CONNEC +

Second and third crosslets low. Last crosslet distant from c. No berries in wreath. A slightly low, its right stand prolonged nearly to U. o partly double cut. I also a little low.   10—E (R⁵)

Obverse 11.

✦ AUCTORI ✦   ✦ CONNEC ✦

Var. 1. First star very close to mail, but not quite touching. Last star touches mail. Stars with five blunt points. Second star distant to left of hair. A inclines decidedly to left.   11¹—E (R²)

Var. 2. First and last stars more distant from mail than in Var. 1. Base of I and second star near hair. Break from upper curve of c to upright of T.   11²—K (R³)

Var. 3. First star touches mail. A leans strongly to left and is very distant from U. U nearly or quite closed. co relatively close. ONN widely spaced. Canfield collection.   11³—K (R⁶)

Obverse 12.

AUCTORI . ✦   CONNEC ✦

Mailed bust left. Twelve leaves in triplets. ONN weakly struck owing to an injury to the die. Period nearly all below I and close to forehead. Upper fillet-end close to final c. Last cinquefoil points between the fillet-ends.   12—Q (R⁴)

Obverse 13.

AUCTORI ✦   ✦ CONNEC ✦

Mailed bust left. Six-pointed stars. Nine leaves and five berries in wreath. UC more closely spaced than the other letters. Break connecting tops of o and R.   13—D (R³)

Obverse 14.

➤ AUCTORI ◄   ➤ ➤ CONNEC. ◄

Mailed bust left. Five pheons in legend. AUCTORI irregularly spaced. Tail of R touches base of I. Uprights of T, R and I all unusually heavy. Upper fillet-end points to period.   14—H (R³)

Obverse 15.

✦ AUCTORI ✦ ✦   ✦ ✦ CONNECT ✦ ✦

Mailed bust left. Seven cinquefoils in legend. Wreath has twelve leaves in triplets; six berries in pairs.   15—F (R³). 15—R (R⁶). 15—S (R⁵)

Draped Busts
Obverse 16.

AUCTORI :   CONNEC :

Type 16 and all the following obverse types of 1787, except 52 and 55, have the bust draped and facing left.

Var. 1. Letters large. A rather near point of bust. Long-tailed R touching base of I. Second C partly on head. O close to head. Last C low. A curved fold of the toga projects from the bust near the lower left corner of A. 16^1—m (R^3)

Var. 2. Letters large. Both colons low. A distant from bust. C close to head, but does not quite touch. Last colon close to final C and end of toga. 16^2—NN^1 (R^4)

Var. 3. Small letters. A very distant from bust. Last colon distant from toga. Top of T slopes to left. 16^3—1^2 (R^4)

Var. 4. Letters large. Both colons low. A very near bust. Last C near fillet-end and in regular position in distinction from Var. 1, where the final C is low.

16^4—n (R^4)

Var. 5. Letters large. First colon distant from hair and a little low. Lower fillet points at last colon. All the C's nearly or quite closed. CONNEC widely spaced. Break from left foot of A, extending into the field. The same A punch was used with Obv. 8 of this year.

In sharp specimens three faint triangularly placed dots occur between the wreath and C. Dr. Hall regards this as accidental and showing little or no evidence of having been made with a punch. 16^5—n (R^3). 16^5—p (R^5). 16^5—u (R^6)

Var. 6. Letters large. A rather distant from bust. Lower dot of first colon very close to hair. AUCTORI widely spaced. C partly on head, O very close or touching head. Top of first N above that of second. C a little low, but not so low as in Var. 1. 16^6—NN^2 (R^6)

Obverse 17.
AUCTORI :   - ✦-CONNEC :

Long-tailed R. Hyphen to right of cross connects with C.   17—g^3 (R^3)

Obverse 18.
AUCTORI : ✦   ✦ CONNEC

Letters small. A distant from bust. NNEC close. Final C connects with toga. Sharp specimens show a period on the toga after the final C.   18—g^1 (R^3)

Obverse 19.
AUCTORI : ✦   ✦ CONNEC :

The letters ORI on a lower plane than AUCT. Long-tailed R. Second cross close to head.   19—g^4 (R^2)

Obverse 20.
AUCTORI : ✱   ✱ CONNEC :

Large letters. A very close to bust. O and I in AUCTORI and final C in CONNEC low. Tail of R connects with base of I. Break from final C in CONNEC to border.

20—a^2 (R^3)

Obverse 21.

AUCTORI : **x**   - **+** - CONNEC : **x**

Letters small. A distant from bust. First cross high. Second cross midway between wreath and C. CO not far from head. Both fillet-ends point at last cross.

In Crosby's table of types Obv. 21 is given with a plain cross without hyphens. Dr. Hall could not find any such die, nor has any specimen of it been since located. In place of it Hall added a new obverse type (54) with hyphens attached to the cross. This seems an unnecessary duplication of types. In worn specimens the hyphens sometimes do not show, but in all other respects the dies are identical.   21—DD (R^4)

Obverse 22.

AUCTORI : **✱**   **+** CONNEC : **x**

Letters small. Top of T leans to left. C touches head, O close. First N double cut. Lower fillet points to last cross.   22—g^2 (R^5)

Obverse 23.

AUCTORI : **+-**   - **+** - CONNEC : - **+** -

Crosby records this obverse combined with his reverse A, but no collection is known to have an example of it. If it exists it is extremely rare.

Obverse 24.

- **+** - AUCTORI :   - **+** - CONNEC :

First O leans to left. R high. Lower dot of first colon partly below I. Upper fillet-end opposite C. Lower fillet points to last colon.

24—g^3 (R^4).   24—g^5 (R^4).   24—FF (R^6)

Obverse 25.

✱ AUCTORI : **x**   ✱ CONNEC :

Large letters. Dots in the angles of first cross. Short hyphen-like lines in angles of cross before CONNEC. Fillets outlined, the lower pointing to colon.

25—b (R^3).   25—m (R^5)

Obverse 26.

✱ AUCTORI :   **x** CONNEC : **✱**

A near point of bust. Letters large. R and I connect. Last cross between ends of toga. In sharp specimens there is a dot between the right arms of the last cross. Breaks through drapery to edge.   26—a^1 (R^5).   26—kk^2 (R^4).   26—AA (R^3)

Obverse 27.

+ AUCTORI : **x**   **x** CONNEC : **x**

Letters large. Imperfect A. Fillet-ends outlined and opposite E and C. EC low. Lower dot of last colon partly on toga. Last star high, opposite end of toga.

27—a^1 (R^5)

Obverse 28.

AUCTORI : **✱**   **✱** CONNEC :

Large letters. Stars with five blunt rays. A near bust. R high. First colon nearly equidistant from I and star. C touches head; O very close. Lower fillet-end points to last colon.   28—m (R^3).   28—n (R^5).   28—o (R^6)

Obverse 29.

AUCTORI : ✢   ✦ CONNEC : ✢

Var. 1.   Large letters.   A touches drapery.   C and O touch head.   First colon low, the lower dot one half below I.   Upper fillet-end points at last colon.   Last star between colon and toga. 29^1—a^2 (R^5). 29^1—n (R^6). 29^1—p (R^4)

Var. 2.   A rather distant from drapery.   I very low.   Second star weak.   C and O touch head.   Four fillet ends, the third opposite last colon.

On some pieces from this die the weak second star is either very rudimentary or does not show.   In his printed list Dr. Hall classified these as type 51, a new obverse. In his later notes he decided this was an error, and changed back the type to 29.

29^2—N (R^6). 29^2—o (R^5)

Obverse 30.

AUCTORI : ✦   ✦ CONNEC : ✦

A midway between bust and U.   Right arm of T above adjoining O.   Second cinquefoil close to head.   Both colons low.   Upper fillet points to last cinquefoil.

30—hh^1 (R^2).   30—X^1 (R^3)

Obverse 31.

✦ AUCTORI : ✦   ✦ CONNEC :

Var. 1.   First cinquefoil close to drapery and mostly to left of it.   A line to left of the upright of T.   I low.   Third cinquefoil nearer to C than to wreath.   C touches head.   Lower fillet-end points to last colon. 31^1—gg^1 (R^3). 31^1—r^4 (R^1)

Var. 2.   First cinquefoil close to point of bust, almost entirely to left of it and about opposite the centre of A.   Tops of R and I on same curve.   C touches head. Lower fillet-end points below last colon.   Break connects third cinquefoil with wreath.

31^2—r^3 (C)

Obverse 32.

✦ AUCTORI . ✦   ✦ CONNEC . ✦

Var. 1.   First cinquefoil half under bust.   Second cinquefoil distant from period and well to left of hair.   Last cinquefoil close to period and toga.   Lower fillet-end points at last period.   Break connects last cinquefoil with end of toga. 32^1—X^3 (R^2)

Var. 2.   First cinquefoil nearly half under bust.   Second cinquefoil near period and distant from hair.   Third cinquefoil distant from head.   Lower fillet points at last cinquefoil.   R and I lean to right.   C touches head, O at medium distance.   Upper fillet-end opposite last period. 32^2—X^1 (C) 32^2—X^2 (R^1). 32^2—X^4 (R^5).

Var. 3.   First cinquefoil about one-fourth under bust.   Second cinquefoil distant from period and most of it above hair.   Third cinquefoil at moderate distance from head.   Last cinquefoil below lower fillet-end.   First period low, below base of I.   Last period opposite lower fillet-end.   Lower line of E imperfect and long.   The E, which is made with an F punch altered, sometimes looks like F.   Final C low. 32^3—X^4 (C)

Var. 4.   First cinquefoil entirely to left of bust.   Second cinquefoil distant from period and much to left of hair.   Third cinquefoil distant from head, and nearly midway between wreath and C.   Last cinquefoil opposite lower fillet-end.   Both periods low, the final one about equidistant from C and cinquefoil.   In CONNEC first C barely touches head.   CO widely spaced, EC close. 32^4—X^5 (R^4). 32^4—Z^3 (R^5)

Var. 5.   First cinquefoil half under bust and very high.   Second cinquefoil low, not far from period and distant from hair.   Third cinquefoil a little distant from head and midway between wreath and c.   Last cinquefoil opposite upper fillet-end and distant from toga.   First period further from ɪ than from cinquefoil.   Last period equidistant from c and cinquefoil.   cт widely spaced.   Right arm of т long.   Final c closed.   Break through final c. 32^5—aa (R^3)

Var. 6.   First cinquefoil entirely to left of bust.   Second cinquefoil low and near period.   Third cinquefoil high and much nearer to wreath than to c.   Last cinquefoil opposite lower fillet-end and distant from toga.   First period low and very close to base of ɪ.   Last period above fillet-end and rather close to c.   Lower right corner of ɪ defective.   ᴇc low. 32^6—X^6 (R^5)

Var. 7.   First cinquefoil about one-fourth under bust and distant from ᴀ.   Second cinquefoil rather near period and distant from hair.   Third cinquefoil high, distant from head.   Lower fillet-end points at last cinquefoil.   First period close to ɪ and cinquefoil, but not so low nor so close to ɪ as in var. 6.   Last period midway between c and cinquefoil.   ʀ a trifle low.   ɪ leans to right.   Defect at top of т.   Final c low.
32^7—X^1 (R^5)

Var. 8.   Letters and cinquefoils large.   Second cinquefoil high, above hair and near period.   Second and third cinquefoils near wreath.   Lower fillet points to edge of last cinquefoil, which is nearer to end of toga than to c.   First period near cinquefoil and opposite hair.   Upper fillet end points just below last period.   Top of ᴀ leans to left.   c clear of head.   No berries in wreath. 32^8—aa (R^5)

Obverse 33.

✶ AUCTORI ! ✶   ✶ CONNEC ! ✶

GROUP I.   Upper fillet-end points at lower dot of last colon :
Varieties 1 to 22.

In each group of this type the varieties are arranged according to the position of the first cinquefoil relative to the point of the bust, the earlier varieties having the cinquefoil entirely, or for the most part, left of the bust; the later varieties with the cinquefoil chiefly or entirely beneath the bust.

In Group I vars. 1 to 9 have the cinquefoil entirely or almost all left of bust.
vars. 10 to 13 have the cinquefoil partly under, but mostly left of bust.
vars. 14 to 18 have the cinquefoil about half under bust.
vars. 19 to 22 have the cinquefoil almost entirely under bust.

Var. 1.   First cinquefoil entirely left of bust, about on a line with the middle of ᴀ.   Second and last cinquefoils close to colons.   Third cinquefoil nearly equidistant from wreath and c.   Colons small and close to ɪ and c.   Upper curve of ᴏʀɪ on lower level than that of ᴀᴜᴄт.   c close to head.   ᴏ rather distant.   ɴɴᴇ high.   Last cinquefoil distant from toga.   Breaks from edge through top of ᴀ to ᴜ; from ɪ through second cinquefoil and hair; from c through top of ᴏ to border; from border to end of toga. 33^1—Z^{13} (R^4). 33^1—Z^{19} (R^5)

Var. 2. First cinquefoil almost wholly left of bust. Second cinquefoil close to forelock. Third cinquefoil close to head and much nearer to C than to wreath. Last cinquefoil rather close to colon and toga. First colon equidistant from I and cinquefoil. Last colon close to C. Medium spacing in AUCTORI, the AU further apart than the other letters. C touches head. O close to head. Second N high. Final C slants to right. In some combinations of this obverse, die-cracks occur along the top and bottom of most of the letters; also from the top of I to the wreath and through the last colon and cinquefoil to the toga.

33^2—Z^5 (C). 33^2—Z^{12} (C). 33^2—Z^{17} (R^4). 33^2—Z^{21} (R^5). 33^2—Z^{22} (R^4)

Var. 3. Cinquefoils: First almost wholly left of bust; second midway between colon and wreath and mostly above hair; third distant from head and a little nearer to C than to wreath; fourth near toga and about twice as far from last colon. First colon wide, the lower dot nearer I. A distant from cinquefoil and U. C partly on head, O very close to head. First N double cut. E from altered F punch. Perfect die; also break from milling through E. In some cases this die-break changes the E into F and makes the legend read CONNFC.

33^3—W^1 (R^3)

Var. 4. Cinquefoils: First close to point of bust, nearly all to left of it; second opposite forelock and nearer colon than wreath; third nearer C than wreath; fourth a little closer to colon than to end of toga. First colon close to I, slanting to right, the lower dot nearer C. Last colon low, the lower dot mostly below C. Letters of AUCTORI irregular, UC and OR more widely spaced than the other letters. C clear of head, O not very distant. In CONNEC both C's low and E double cut. Break through AUCTO to milling. Another through lower part of bust to milling.

33^4—q (R^4). 33^4—Z^2 (R^5)

Var. 5. First cinquefoil close to bust, almost entirely to left of it; second a little distant from forelock and midway between colon and wreath; third clear of head and about equidistant from wreath and C; fourth equally distant from upper dot of last colon and toga. First colon wide, nearer to I than to cinquefoil. Last colon low, the lower dot mostly below C. A slightly high. C touches head. O close to head. Final C low. Die crack along top of AUC.

33^5—T^2 (R^3)

Var. 6. First cinquefoil considerably below point of bust and almost entirely to left of it; second distant to left of hair and midway between colon and wreath; third high, distant from head and a little nearer to C than to wreath. First colon slanting, the lower dot nearer to I and distant from cinquefoil. Last colon wide, near to C and cinquefoil, which is high, and opposite the upper dot of the colon. The letters RI slope to right. C close to head. O somewhat distant. CON widely spaced. Three fillet ends. Toga double cut.

33^6—KK (R^1)

Var. 7. First cinquefoil about three-fourths left of bust and distant from A; second opposite upper dot of colon and nearer to it than to wreath; third high, nearer to C than to wreath; fourth mostly beyond end of toga and equally distant from colon and toga. Dots of both colons heavy and close. Lower dot of first colon about half below the base of I. Legend well spaced. C low, almost touching head, O distant. Break through upright of T.

33^7—r^2 (C). 33^7—r^4 (R^6). 33^7—Z^{10} (R^6)

Var. 8.   First cinquefoil one-fourth under bust and high, distant from A; second fairly distant from colon and hair; third rather distant from head, nearer C than to wreath; last midway between colon and toga.   First colon close to I, the lower dot touching the base of that letter.   Last colon a little nearer C than to cinquefoil.   R high, leaning to right.   Irregularity in die at right of I making the I thick and blurred. C clear of head, but close to it.   O distant from head.   E high, the top leaning to right. Breaks from milling to A and E. 33^8—Z^{13} (R^4). 33^8—Z^{19} (R^5)

Var. 9.   First cinquefoil close to bust and about three-fourths to left of it; second distant from colon and well to left of hair; third distant from head and about equidistant from wreath and C; last cinquefoil nearer to end of toga than to colon.   Upper dot of both colons low.   C clear of head, O distant.   Break from milling through first C.   In some cases other die breaks, especially through last colon to lower fillet.
$$33^9\text{—}s^2 \text{ (R}^2\text{)}$$

Var. 10.   First cinquefoil high, partly under bust, but mostly to left of it; second partly over and very close to hair; third near wreath; last distant from colon and very close to end of toga.   First colon low, nearly midway between I and cinquefoil.   Last colon in regular position, a little nearer to C than to cinquefoil.   First O low.   CO low and touching head.   ON widely spaced.
$$33^{10}\text{—}Z^7 \text{ (R}^5\text{)}.   33^{10}\text{—}Z^8 \text{ (R}^4\text{)}.   33^{10}\text{—}W^6 \text{ (R}^6\text{)}$$

Var. 11.   First cinquefoil high, more than half to left of bust; second near colon, partly over and near hair; third close to head, and nearer to C than wreath; last cinquefoil low, midway between colon and end of toga.   First colon low, a little nearer to I than to cinquefoil.   Last colon not far from C.   AUCTORI widely spaced.   C touches head, O well clear of it.   Top of E leans to right.   Break over TO.   Break from milling to upper fillet. 33^{11}—Z^{18} (R^4). 33^{11}—gg^1 (R^5)

Var. 12.   First cinquefoil high, more than half to left of bust; second distant from colon and hair; third high, nearer C than wreath; last close to toga, the upper part in line with upper dot of colon.   First colon low, the lower dot half below I and nearer to I than to cinquefoil.   AUCTORI well spaced, with T high and I low.   C very close to or touching head.   O very close to C and distant from N.   Break from first cinquefoil through AUCTO; also from milling through E.
$$33^{12}\text{—}W^3 \text{ (R}^5\text{)}.   33^{12}\text{—}Z^{16} \text{ (R}^3\text{)}.   33^{12}\text{—}Z^{21} \text{ (R}^5\text{)}.   33^{12}\text{—}Z^{24} \text{ (R}^6\text{)}$$

Var. 13.   First cinquefoil low, nearly half under and touching bust; second very low and almost touching lower dot of colon; third also low, touching head; last midway between final colon and end of toga.   Colon dots close, the upper dot of both colons low and close to letters.   A closer than usual to first cinquefoil and bust.   C on head, O very close to head.   Semi-circular break over O in AUCTORI, connecting with upper corner of T.   Break from milling through fillets, sometimes closing the final C.
33^{13}—Z^1 (R^5). 33^{13}—Z^6 (R^4). 33^{13}—Z^7 (R^4). 33^{13}—q (R^5). 33^{13}—ff^1 (R^6).
$$33^{13}\text{—}hh^2 \text{ (R}^6\text{)}$$

Var. 14.   First cinquefoil about half under bust; second high, distant from colon and partly above forelock; third distant from head, nearer to C than wreath; last high, mostly above end of toga and rather nearer to toga than to colon.   Colons distant from letters and cinquefoils. Letters CO close to head, but do not touch. EC more closely spaced than other letters. A curved die-break, starting below the drapery, runs through the first cinquefoil and along the top of AUCT to the milling above first colon. Crack from point of bust to milling. 33^{14}— Z^{14} (R^3)

Var. 15. Cinquefoils: first half under bust and very distant from A; second high, opposite upper dot of colon, distant from colon and hair; third high, midway between C and wreath; fourth distant from colon, close to toga and mostly above it. Colon dots heavy and rather close. First colon low, the lower dot largely below I, but closer than the upper dot to I. Last colon near C. Top of R above top of O. CO clear of head. Top of second N leans to right. NNE high. 33^{15}—r^1 (R^1)

Var. 16. Second N double cut. Otherwise same die as var. 14. Breaks from milling to lower end of toga and from milling to last cinquefoil.

$$33^{16}—1^2 \ (R^4). \quad 33^{16}—Z^{15} \ (R^1). \quad (36^{16}—T^2) \ R^6$$

Var. 17. First cinquefoil half under bust and a little more distant from it than in var. 15; second cinquefoil high, a trifle over but not so far from hair as in var. 15. Third cinquefoil not very distant from head. Last cinquefoil nearly all above end of toga and well separated from it. Base of I trifle below R. In other respects this die closely resembles var. 15, differing chiefly in the position of the second and third cinquefoils, which are nearer to the hair than in var. 15.

$$33^{17}—r^1 \ (R^3). \quad 33^{17}—r^5 \ (R^6). \quad 33^{17}—gg^2 \ (R^2)$$

Var. 18. First cinquefoil about half under bust and close to drapery; second distant from colon, hair and wreath; third high, distant from head and a little nearer to C than to wreath; last cinquefoil about equidistant from colon and toga. First colon thus ⁚ , slanting to right, the lower dot nearly all below I and nearer than the upper dot to I. Last colon also low, the dots close, and midway between C and last cinquefoil. AUCTORI rather closely and about evenly spaced, with A and I a little low. Letters small. C touches head, O low and very close to head. Top of first N above that of second. This obverse is not in Hall's list. 33^{18}—Z^{24} (R^6)

Var. 19. First cinquefoil close to bust and almost wholly under it; second very close to colon and distant from hair; third high; last close to colon and toga. Both colons low and close to letters and cinquefoils. A nearer to bust than to cinquefoil. I low and double cut. (The double cutting does not show when this obverse is combined with Rev. q.) C touches head, O distant. Base line of E defective, the punch probably altered from F. Final C low, slanting to right.

$$33^{19}—Z^1 \ (C). \quad 33^{19}—Z^2 \ (R^3). \quad 33^{19}—q \ (R^5)$$

Var. 20. First cinquefoil almost entirely below drapery and very distant from A; second partly over and distant from hair, its centre on a line with upper dot of colon and nearer to colon than to hair; third midway between wreath and C; last nearer to end of toga than to colon. First colon wide, nearly equidistant from I and cinquefoil, the lower dot partly below I. Last colon nearer to C than to cinquefoil. Tops of R and I lean to right. C and O touch head and are widely spaced. O in CONNEC low. Final C low. 33^{20}—Z^9 (R^4). 33^{20}—Z^{11} (R^6)

Var. 21. Not in Hall's list, but given in his later notes as follows:

"Colons heavy, the lower periods about half below adjacent letters. AU and CT closer than the other letters in AUCTORI. CONNEC widely spaced, except NE. End of toga defective, giving the appearance of two small periods following the last cinquefoil."

Two specimens of this obverse have been located. 33^{21}—Z^{13} (R^6)

Var. 22. First cinquefoil partly below bust and closer to A than usual. AUCTORI widely spaced, UC closer than the other letters. Second cinquefoil low, its centre on a line with lower dot of colon. Last cinquefoil low, nearer colon than end of toga. Last colon low and close to C. I over an O. C close to head. 33^{22}—II (R^6)

The only specimen known is in the collection of Mr. Hillyer Ryder. The fillet-ends are not clear enough to decide whether it should be placed in the first or second group.

Obverse 33 continued.

GROUP II. IN VARIETIES 23 TO 28 INCLUSIVE, THE UPPER FILLET-END POINTS BETWEEN THE LAST COLON AND CINQUEFOIL.

In varieties 23 to 25 the first cinquefoil is entirely left of bust.
In variety 26 the first cinquefoil is about one-half under bust.
In varieties 27 and 28 the first cinquefoil is more than half under bust.

Var. 23. The first cinquefoil entirely to left of bust; second cinquefoil distant from colon and near hair; third high; last nearly midway between colon and toga. First colon low, the dots close and not far from I. Last colon near C. AUCT widely spaced. U slopes to left, its top above that of C. C touches head, O very close. NE high. E leans to right. 33^{23}—Z^4 (R^2). 33^{23}—hh^2 (R^5)

Var. 24. First cinquefoil entirely to left of bust. Top of U on same curve as adjoining C. C on head. CO closely spaced. E low. 33^{24}—Z^{10} (R^6)

Var. 25. First cinquefoil entirely to left of bust; second partly above forelock and nearer to it than to colon; third high; last distant both from colon and toga. Both colons a little low and distant from letters, the colon dots heavy. AUCTORI widely spaced. T a trifle high. C almost touching, O rather near head. NNE high. Break from neck to milling. Crack from lower fillet through edge of last cinquefoil.
    33^{25}—W^3 (R^5). 33^{25}—Z^{10} (R^4). 33^{25}—Z^{24} (R^5)

Var. 26. First cinquefoil half under, nearly touching bust; second very near, or touching hair; second and third both near wreath; last cinquefoil opposite and near lower fillet-end, distant from toga. A very high, top sloping to left. O in CONNEC low and well on head. N above adjacent O. Heavy break across lower portion of drapery. 33^{26}—W^3 (R^5). 33^{26}—W^5 (R^6)

Var. 27. First cinquefoil more than half under bust and very close to drapery; second distant from colon and hair; third low, close to head; last cinquefoil a little nearer to end of toga than to colon. Colons in regular position, the first midway between I and cinquefoil, the last not far from C. Letters small. OR widely spaced. R and I lean to right. In CONNEC the EC closer than other letters. Break from nose to upright of R. 33^{27}—Z^{16} (R^6). 33^{27}—r^4 (R^4)

Var. 28. First cinquefoil most all under bust, below the drapery; second distant from colon and hair; third high; last about midway between C and toga, which ends in two heavy dots. Colons nearer to letters than to cinquefoils. Letters small. C close to, or touching, O near head. Base line of E long. Letters NEC rather close at bottom. Break from second N through head and nose to milling. (This break does not show when combined with Rev. Z^{20}.)

$$33^{28}—Z^{11} \ (R^3). \quad 33^{28}—Z^{16} \ (R^3). \quad 33^{28}—Z^{20} \ (R^6)$$

Obverse 33 continued.

GROUP III. IN VARIETIES 29 TO 41, THE LOWER FILLET-END POINTS AT THE LAST COLON.

In varieties 29 to 34 inclusive the first cinquefoil is entirely or almost entirely left of the bust.

In varieties 35 to 39 the first cinquefoil is partly under the bust, but mostly left of it.

In variety 40 the cinquefoil is half under the bust; in 41 entirely under.

Var. 29. First cinquefoil entirely under bust and nearer A than usual; second, opposite space between colon dots and not far from hair; third, clear of head, nearer to C than to wreath. Last cinquefoil touches end of toga. First colon sloping, thus ∴, the lower dot almost all below I. Last colon near C and a little further from the cinquefoil, the upper dot low. Letters large. Broad I, its base a little below the curve of OR. C on head, O distant. First N high. Top of E leans to right. Die-cracks in front of mouth and downward from chin. Sometimes other cracks through C to fillets and from edge through toga and drapery to neck. These cracks especially occur in the combination with reverse Z. $33^{29}—Z^7 \ (R^4). \quad 33^{29}—gg^1 \ (R^4)$

Var. 30. First cinquefoil very high, entirely left of bust; second above hair, its top on about the same curve as the tops of I and wreath; third distant from head, slightly nearer to C than to wreath; last high, near end of toga and distant from colon. First colon midway between I and cinquefoil. Upper dot of last colon weak, the lower dot below C. A slightly high, its top leaning to left. Upper curve of TORI on lower plane than that of AUC. U nearly closed at top. I broad and low. CO clear of head.

$$33^{30}—EE \ (R^5). \quad 33^{30}—SS \ (R^6)$$

Var. 31. First cinquefoil below point of bust and entirely left of it; second distant from colon and not far to left of hair; third, close to head and nearer C than usual; last cinquefoil nearly touches end of toga. Lower dot of first colon close to I. Last colon midway between C and cinquefoil, the upper dot low. AU and CT relatively wide. I low. C touches head, O distant. Last C slants to right. $33^{31}—gg^2 \ (R^5)$

Var. 32. First cinquefoil entirely left of bust, its top on a level with the top of A; second near hair; third close to head and near C; fourth close to end of toga, about twice as far from colon. First colon slanting to right, the lower dot nearer I. Lower dot of last colon heavy, partly below C. ORI closely spaced. I heavy and low. C touches head, O distant. Left part of first N closed. E double cut. Final C very low.

Some examples show die-cracks from second cinquefoil through lower dot of colon and along base of I; from left of A through first cinquefoil to milling; from milling through drapery; in the field before face and bust. 33^{32}—Z^{13} (R^1)

Var. 33. First cinquefoil beyond point of bust, between drapery and A; second midway between colon and wreath, partly over hair; third not far from head, a little nearer C than wreath; fourth between end of toga and milling and very close to toga. First colon very low, the lower dot much below the base of I. Last colon widely spaced, the upper dot partly above the top of C. Small letters. U high, top of O leans to left. C touches, O close to head. CT and ON widely spaced.

On some specimens there is a slight crack downward from the eye along middle of nose; another also from top of wreath to milling. 33^{33}—Z^3 (R^4). 33^{33}—Z^{11} (R^3)

Var. 34. First cinquefoil close to point of bust and nearly all to left of it; second above hair, midway between upper dot of colon and wreath; third high; fourth opposite space between colon dots and very close to end of toga. Colons with large, heavy dots, the lower dot of first colon partly below I. Last colon wide, equidistant from C and cinquefoil. UCT, ORI, and ONNE widely spaced. Left arm of T defective. C partly on head. O close to head and nearer to C than to N. NNE high, close to milling. Final C very low.

Break from wreath to milling; also between the tops of O and N.
33^{34}—W^2 (R^5). 33^{34}—Z^3 (R^5). 33^{34}—Z^{11} (R^5)

Var. 35. First cinquefoil nearly touching bust and about three-quarters left of it. Second and fourth cinquefoils near colons. R high, its top sloping to right. Second N high. Wide spacing between N and E. EC close. The tail of R is long, apparently an alteration.

Break from lower part of bust through tops of letters AUCTO to milling over R. Heavy break near upper left corner of R. 33^{35}—Z^9 (R^6)

Var. 36. First cinquefoil about three-quarters beyond bust and well clear of it; second close to colon and distant to left from hair; third high, nearer to C than to wreath; last opposite space between colon dots, and nearly equidistant from colon and end of toga. Colons wide, in regular position. Letters small. In AUCTORI O and R lean to right. I high. C touches head. O at medium distance, leaning to left. NN high. Lower line of E heavy and long.
33^{36}—T^1 (R^3). 33^{36}—T^2 (R^1). 33^{36}—SS (R^6)

Var. 37. First cinquefoil about three-fourths beyond bust; second above hair, equidistant from colon and wreath; third close to head, nearer C than wreath; fourth mostly above upper dot of colon and end of toga and quite close to the toga. First colon distant from I and cinquefoil, the upper dot low. Last colon very low, the lower dot entirely below C. Letters widely spaced. A and I low. Period after O in AUCTORI. C partly on head. O high. E from an F punch altered clumsily, the base line too short. Final C low. A heavy dot at the milling, between last colon and cinquefoil. 33^{37}—Z^9 (R^3)

Var. 38. First cinquefoil below bust and more than half to left of it; second near and partly over hair, a little closer to upper dot of colon than to wreath; third

nearer c than wreath; last midway between colon and end of toga. Upper dot of
colon low. AU more widely spaced than other letters. The letters ORI slope to right.
O in CONNEC low. C close to head, but does not touch. Final c large and low.

Break from first cinquefoil along bottom of AUCT and through o to milling.
Other breaks from milling downward through first colon, and from milling through
upright of R to nose. With some reverses there is a curved break from left of A to
milling. 33^{38}—Z^1 (R^3). 33^{38}—Z^6 (R^4). 33^{38}—Z^{23} (R^5). 33^{38}—gg^1 (R^5).

Var. 39.   First cinquefoil close to bust and more than half to left of it; second
distant from colon and hair; third distant from head, much nearer to c than to wreath;
last very close to end of toga. Colons close, the upper dot of both low. AUC more
widely spaced than other letters in AUCTORI. Top of first o leans to right. CO widely
spaced. C well clear of head. O distant from head. 33^{39}—Z^{20} (R^6). 33^{39}—s^1 (C).

Var. 40.   First cinquefoil one-half or more under bust; second high, opposite
upper dot of colon, distant from colon, hair and wreath; third very high, distant from
head, wreath and c; fourth not far from colon, opposite upper dot. First colon nearer I
than cinquefoil, but distant from both. Last colon near c, the dots close, the upper
one low. AU widely spaced. C touches head, o distant. EC close. Break from milling through centre of A. Heavy break from end of toga and last cinquefoil to milling.
          33^{40}—Z^1 (R^5). 33^{40}—Z^2 (R^5)

Var. 41.   First cinquefoil very far under bust and very distant from A; second
distant from colon and hair; third distant from head, wreath and c; last cinquefoil
opposite and close to end of toga. Dots of both colons small, the upper ones low.
Letters small. UC and EC closer than other letters. C just touches head. O high,
leaning to left. Wide spacing in ONNE. Heavy break from head across neck and
drapery to milling. Crack from milling along left side of I to nose. 33^{41}—Z^{11} (R^6)

Obverse 33 continued

GROUP IV.   In Variety 42 the lower fillet-end points at the last cinquefoil;
    in varieties 43 to 45 both fillet-ends point at last cinquefoil.

Var. 42.   First cinquefoil entirely left of bust. Second high, very near upper
dot of first colon. Last cinquefoil opposite lower fillet-end. Both colons sloping, the
upper dot nearer letters. Highest portion of upper fillet-end opposite right edge of
final c. Last c low. 33^{42}—Z^2 (R^6)

Var. 43.   First cinquefoil close to point of bust and wholly to left of it; second
to left of hair, distant both from colon and hair; third nearer wreath than c; fourth
midway between colon and end of toga and distant from both. Upper dot of both
colons low. C touches, o very close to head. Second N high. ON and NE widely
spaced. EC close. 33^{43}—q (R^4). 33^{43}—hh^2 (R^4)

Var. 44.   First cinquefoil very high, above the top of A and about three-fourths
left of bust; second very close to forelock; third touches head. Last cinquefoil distant from colon, fillet-ends and toga. First colon wide, midway between I and cinquefoil. Last colon low, the lower dot below c. AUCTORI widely spaced. C touches
head, o close.

Break from milling through drapery to A, and from milling through o in CONNEC.

44⁴⁴—W³ (R⁵)

Var. 45. First cinquefoil about half under bust, distant from A; second distant from colon, near forelock and partly above it; third touching head; last distant from toga and fully twice as far from colon. First colon wide, the lower dot nearer I. Lower dot of last colon a little low. Wide spacing in AUCTORI except between U and C. Top of T above that of C. C in CONNEC touches head and is nearer to wreath than usual. O near head. Final C low.

33⁴⁵—W² (R⁵)

1787

Obverse 34.

AUCTORI : ⟵   ⟶ CONNEC : ⟵

The only die with large fleurons. First fleuron touches forelock.

34—k³ (R⁶).   34 ff¹ (R³)

Obverse 35.

AUCTORI : ⟵   ⟶ CONNEC : ⟵

Small fleurons. Crosby gives this obverse combined with his reverse F. Dr. Hall could not find this die. All supposed examples proved on close examination to be obverse dies of Type 37 with the first fleuron weakly struck or worn off by circulation.

Obverse 36.

⟶ AUCTORI : ⟵   ⟶ CONNEC :

Small fleurons. First fleuron about half under bust. Both C's in CONNEC low. Lower fillet-end points to last colon.

36—k³ (R⁵).   36 l¹ (R³).   36—ff² (R⁵)

Obverse 37.

⟶ AUCTORI : ⟵   ⟶ CONNEC : ⟵

First fleuron entirely left of bust. Varieties 1 and 2.
First fleuron mostly left of bust. Varieties 3 to 7.
First fleuron half under bust. Varieties 8 to 10.
First fleuron mostly under bust. Variety 11.
First fleuron entirely under bust. Varieties 12 to 14.

Var. 1 Fleurons: first left of bust; second distant from colon; third clear of head, nearer C than wreath; fourth close to end of toga. First colon nearer to I than to fleuron. Last colon about equidistant from C and final fleuron, the lower dot of the colon nearer I. I low. CO clear of head. Lower fillet points at last colon.

37¹—cc¹ (R²)

Var. 2. Fleurons: first almost entirely left of bust; second distant from colon, hair and wreath; third close to head; fourth midway between final colon and toga. First colon sloping, the lower dot nearer I and about one half below that letter. Last colon also sloping to right and opposite upper fillet end. AUCT widely spaced, with U out of position and high. C touches head, O not far from head. Final C low and imperfect. Lower fillet points at last fleuron. Break through AUCTO.

37²—k⁵ (R³)

Var. 3. Fleurons: first close to bust, partly under, but mostly left; second distant from colon, very close to hair; third not far from head, and nearer c than wreath; fourth near colon and toga. Both colons slightly low and well separated from letters. Long tailed R. Top of I leans to right. E high, leaning to right. Lower fillet points at last fleuron. 37^3—i (R^2)

Var. 4. Fleurons: first partly under, but more than half to left of bust; second distant from colon and hair; third very close to head; last distant from colon and end of toga. First colon distant from I. Last colon rather distant from c. T above o. I low. Second N above the first. c low. 37^4—k^1 (R^1). 37^4—RR (R^6)

Var. 5. Fleurons: first close to bust, and more than half to left of it; second distant from colon and hair; third near head; last about midway between colon and end of toga. Upper dot of first colon low and distant from I. Last colon low, well separated from c and fleuron. Long tailed R. c touches head, o very close. First N high.

Break from milling to head between third fleuron and c. A later break through second fleuron. 37^5—e (R^2)

Var. 6. Fleurons: first near bust, more than half to left of it; second near, but clear of hair; third clear of head, and closer to c than to wreath; last rather closer to end of toga than to upper dot of colon. First colon sloping, the upper dot more distant from I. Last colon very low, the lower dot mostly below c. Long tailed R. c on head, o rather close. Second N high. Final c low. Upper curved line of drapery extends nearly to ribbon bow. 37^6—k^4 (R^4). 37^6—B (R^6)

Var. 7. Fleurons: first more than half left of bust and almost touching it; last fleuron near toga. Dots of first colon equidistant from I. Three berries in wreath. T high. 37^7—h^2 (R^5)

Var. 8. Fleurons: first about half under and clear of bust; second near colon, a little further from hair; third close to head and much nearer to c than to wreath; last fleuron close to colon and end of toga. Colons well apart from letters. Last colon points at low part of upper fillet-end. UC and OR widely spaced. I low. c on head. o close to head. Crack from drapery along the bottom of AU. Another through third fleuron and top of wreath to upper dot of first colon.

.37^8—k^2 (R^2). 37^8—HH (R^3). 37^8—LL (R^3)

Var. 9. Fleurons: first half under bust; second very distant from colon and distant to left of hair; third well above head and midway between wreath and c; last distant from colon and toga. Both fillet-ends point to last fleuron. Colons well spaced and nearer to the letters than to the fleurons. Last colon above the upper fillet-end. c close to head, but clear of it and much nearer to wreath than usual. Left lower curve of o quite close to head. Last c very low. Three berries in wreath. 37^9—e (R^3)

Var. 10. Fleurons: first half under and close to bust; second distant from upper dot of colon and considerably to left of hair; third nearer to c than to top of wreath; last distant slightly from colon and toga. Both colons sloping to right, the lower dots nearer the letters. Lower dot of last colon one half below c. c touches head, o somewhat distant. Last c low.

A slight die-crack is found from the top of U to the left arm of T. 37^{10}—RR (R^4)

Var. 11. Fleurons: first more than half under bust; second distant from colon and hair; third close to head; last a little further from space between colon dots than from end of toga. First colon low. The dots of last colon nearer to c than to fleuron. AUCTORI widely spaced. A near bust. c touches head. o very close to head. Lower corner of N very distant from head. CON widely spaced. Final c low.

37^{11}—ff^2 (R^3)

Var. 12. Fleurons: first entirely under bust, touching drapery; second distant from colon and hair; third close to head, about half way between wreath and c; last low, midway between lower dot of colon and toga. Both colons sloping, the lower dots nearer letters. Legend widely spaced. U defective at upper left corner. Long tailed R. c touches head, o very close to head, leaning to left. The upper curved line of the drapery extends back of the neck up to the ribbon bow.

37^{12}—LL (R^4). 37^{12}—TT (R^5)

Var. 13. Fleurons: first wholly under bust, distant from A; second close to upper dot of colon, distant from hair; third well separated from head; last close to space between colon dots and pointing to lower edge of upper dot. First colon slopes decidedly to right, with the lower dot much the nearer to I. Last colon slightly low, the lower dot about half way between c and fleuron. R high and above o. R and I lean to right. c on head. o close to head, leaning to left and distant from N. Legend widely spaced.

Die cracks through middle of last c, and from bottom of c to toga. 37^{13}—HH (R^2)

Var. 14. Fleurons: first high entirely under bust; slightly distant from colon, pointing between the dots; third close to head; last distant from colon and low, pointing at lower dot of colon. Both colons low and sloping to right. Wide spacing in AUCTORI. c touches head. Upper fillet-end opposite space between last colon and fleuron. Lower fillet end points at last fleuron. A curved fold of the toga extends from point of bust uniting with the first fleuron. 37^{14}—cc^2 (R^6)

Obverse 38.

AUCIORI :   + CONNEC: x

AUCI widely spaced, ORI closer. Colons wide. Large letters.

38—GG (R^2).   38—l^2 (R^3)

Obverse 39.

→ AUCTOBI : ←   → CONNEC : ←

Var. 1. First fleuron almost entirely under bust. Third fleuron close to head. Last colon low, the lower dot below c. Three berries in wreath. Medium spacing.

39^1—ff^2 (R^5).   39^1—h^1 (R^5)

Var. 2. First fleuron half under bust. Second fleuron distant from colon, pointing between the dots. First colon sloping, the lower dot much nearer I. Last colon regular. Milling coarse.   39^2—ee (R^4)

Obverse 40.

AUCTOPI ✦   ✦ CONNEC

Large letters. Stars with five blunt points. Last c touches end of toga. In most specimens the space between A and U is incused, showing a small raised letter like a c.

40—N (R^5).   40—kk^1 (R^5)

Obverse 41.

✿ AUCTOPI : ✿   ✿ CONNEC :

Large letters. Stars with five blunt points. Upper dot of colon after I very low. Last fillet end opposite c. Lower dot of colon on end of toga.

Crosby and Hall give the final punctuation of the legend as a period. Sharp specimens indicate that it is more likely a colon, the lower dot touching and blending with the end of the toga adjacent to c.   41—ii (R³)

Obverse 42.

✿ AUCTOPI :   ✿ CONNEC · ✿

Large letters. Stars with five blunt points. First star partly under bust. I and upper dot of colon low. Period close to end of toga. Last star below drapery.

As in Obverse 41 the final punctuation may have been meant for a colon, the lower dot weak and blending with the end of the toga. However this is not so clearly shown as in Obverse 41. Break from milling to wreath.   42—o (R⁶). 42—kk² (R²)

Obverse 43.

✿ AUCTORI . ✿   ✿ CONNFC . ✿

Letters small and closely spaced except co. Cinquefoils near periods. c touches head, o very close to head. F punch used for E. Upper fillet-end points at last cinquefoil.   43—Y (C)

Obverse 44.

✿ AUCTORI :   ✿ CONNEC : ✿

First cinquefoil close to point of bust and most all to left of it. No cinquefoil between colon and wreath. Last cinquefoil close to toga. Lower dot of first colon close to hair. AUCT widely spaced. Top of ORI on a lower curve than that of AUCT. c partly on head. E made with an F punch altered. EC consecutively low.

    44—W⁴ (R²). 44—W⁵ (R⁵). 44—Z¹⁰ (R⁵)

Obverse 45.

-✖- AUCTORI : -✚-   -✖- CONNEC : -✚-

Small letters. Cross with hyphens before AUCTORI. Hyphen to left of second cross joins the cross. Last cross between ends of toga. Second N high. Lower fillet-end points at last colon.   45—CC (R⁴)

Obverse 46.

✿ AUCTORI : ✖ -   -✖- CONNEC : -✖-

First cross below bust and high. Good specimens show dots in three angles of this cross instead of the plain cross in Dr. Hall's list. Second cross high. The hyphen to right of this cross touches wreath. Last cross between the ends of the toga. Colons wide. Letters large. A close to bust. The tail of R joins the base line of I. EC low. Last colon distant from toga.   46—BB (R⁴)

Obverse 47.

❋ AUCTORI : - ✖ -   - ✖ - CONNEC :

Large letters. Leaves of wreath outlined. The tail of R does not join I. Three fillet-ends opposite c.

47—a³ (R⁵)

Obverse 48.

→ AUCTORI : ↞•   ••→ CONNEC : ↞

First fleuron slightly under bust; last distant from toga. Upper fillet points at last colon. ON widely spaced. The periods after second and before third fleuron distinguish this legend from Obv. 37.

48—g⁵ (R⁵)

Obverse 49.

✦ AUCTORI : ✦   ✦ ✦ CONNEC : ✦

Two cinquefoils between the wreath and c, as in Obv. 15. Two known.

49—Z¹ (R⁶)

Obverse 50.

✦ AUCTORI . ✦   ✦ CONNLC . ✦

First cinquefoil between drapery and A; second close to colon and hair. Last cinquefoil between ends of toga. Letters large. Both fillet-ends point to c. Same die as Obv. 17 of 1788. Irregular die-cracks in front of face and neck, one passing through first c to milling.

50—F (R⁵)

Obverse 51.

AUCTORI ✦   CONNEC ✦

This obv. given by Dr. Hall, but later changed by him to obv. 29². Sharp, well struck specimens show an additional star, weakly struck, before CONNEC. This renders the legend identical with that of Obv. 29. The combination is 29²—o.

Obverse 52.

AUCTORI :   CONNEC :

Mailed bust, facing right. Head of medium size and round, with Roman nose. Fillet-ends tied with a bow.

52—G

Obverse 53.

→ AUCTORI : ↞   •→ CONNEC : ↞

First fleuron low, slightly under bust. Second fleuron also low. Last fleuron distant from colon and toga. Upper dot of last colon the nearer to c.

The period before third fleuron distinguishes this legend from those of Obverses 37 and 48.

53—FF (R⁴)

Obverse 54.

AUCTORI : ✖   - ✦ - CONNEC : ✖

Legend the same as Crosby's Obv. 21 with hyphens added to the second cross. All specimens examined of Type 21 prove to be identical with Hall's 54, with the hyphens weakly struck or worn off. This die, therefore, has been listd as Obv. 21 with hyphens added to Crosby's legend.

Obverse 55.

❀ AUCTORI . ❀   ❀ CONNEC . ❀

Mailed bust, facing left. Same legend as obverse 32. Mule of obv. 16 of 1788.

55—F (R⁶)

1787 REVERSE

Reverse A

ETLIB   INDE

Coarse, serrated milling. Large Liberty cap.   1¹—A

Reverse B.

INDE   ET   LIB

Large letters. Coarse milling, most of it wanting. Branch points at lower left corner of E in ET.   2—B. 37⁶—B

Reverse C.

INDE • ET   LIB

Period after INDE large. Date small, figures leaning to left, short branch with three leaves. Elbow forms a sharp point.   1²—C

Reverse D.

⁺ INDE ₊ ET ₊ ₊   ₊   ₊ LIB ₊ ₊

Two crosslets between ET and head. The curved lower end of the shield terminates in a crosslet. Left upright of N double cut.   9—D. 13—D

Reverse E.

❀ INDE ❀ ET ❀   ❀ LIB ❀ ❀

Stars with five blunt points. Plume projecting from hair-knot, wide spacing between I B.   9—E. 10—E. 11¹—E

Reverse F.

❀ INDE ❀ ET ❀ ❀   ❀   ❀ LIB ❀ ❀

Eight cinquefoils in legend, the first weak and close to foot of Liberty. The last cinquefoil close to shield. Coarse, serrated milling.   15—F. 50—F. 55—F

Reverse G

INDE ❀ ET   LIB ❀

Stars with six sharp points. Last star near B, distant from shield. 3—G. 52—G

Reverse H.

INDE • ET   →   → LIB. ◄◄

Small date. A pheon on each side of date. Top of T in ET weak.   14—H

Reverse I.

INDE : ⁘   ET LIB.

Lower and right dots of group connect. ET widely spaced. Break in the die between D and E.   7—I

Reverse K.

✷ INDE ✷   ✷ ET LIB ✷

Stars with five blunt points. Plume from hair-knot. INDE widely spaced. Stars somewhat distant from foot and shield.   11²—K. 11³—K

Reverse L.

INDE •   ET • LIB •

Letters large with wide spacing. Top leaf of branch below lower right corner of E.

1³—L. 4—L

Reverse M.

INDE : ✷ ✷   ✷ ET • LIB :

Stars with six blunt points. Liberty cap low. All figures of date distant from date line.   6¹—M. 6²—M

Reverse N.

INDE ✷ ✷   ✷ ETLIB ✷

Stars with five blunt points. Branch points at first star. Last star close to lower part of shield. Figure 8 imperfect.   8—N. 29²—N. 40—N

Reverse O.

✷ INDE : ✷ ✷   ✷ ETLIB : ✷

Stars with five blunt points. D smaller than other letters in INDE. Lower line of L long and close to base of I.   8—O

Reverse P.

• IN DE •   ET LIB •

The first two periods opposite the centre of letters; the last period high. Branch between N and D. The lower right corner of B disconnected and extending to right. In date 17 low.   5—P

Reverse Q.

✿ IN DE •   ETLIB • ✿

Both periods low. Last period and cinquefoil partly in shield. Branch hand between N and D. Branch points at upper part of upright of D. Coarse milling. 12—Q

Reverse R.

✤ IND ˣ ˣ   ✤ ET ✤   ˣ ✤ ✤ LIB ✤   ✤ ˣ

Eleven crosslets in legend. The lower curved portion of the shield terminates in a crosslet as in reverse D. Leaves of branch made with the same crosslet punch. Coarse milling. Irregular die-break to left of last 7 of date, giving the 7 the appearance of having been struck over an 8.   9—R. 15—R

Reverse S.

✿ INDL ✿ ET ✿   ✿ LIB ✿

Besides the cinquefoils in the legend, a cinquefoil is shown on each side of the date. The one on the left is distant from the figure 1 and touches the line. The cinquefoil on the right is below the line and close to the top of 7. In the date I is distant from 7 and leans decidedly to left.

A heavy break from right edge of shield to border nearly obliterates the letters IB. The few specimens known of this very rare die are all in poor condition.   15—S

Reverse T.

⚬ INDE : ⚬ ⚬   ⚬ ETLIB : ⚬

Var. 1. Lower dot of last colon distant from shield. No terminal leaf to branch. Date-line single.

Heavy break from edge near last cinquefoil. Break from milling between edge and fourth cinquefoil. 33^{36}—T^1

Var. 2. Lower dot of last colon touches shield. "Skeleton hand." Date-line double. 33^5—T^2. 33^{16}—T^2. 33^{36}—T^2

Reverse V.

⚬ INDE . ⚬ ⚬ ⚬   ⚬ ET LIB ⚬

This die is given in Crosby's table in combination with obv. 32. Dr. Hall also includes it in his list, but his record of the number of pieces of each variety found contains no examples of Rev. V except two, both of which he later erased from his list. It seems reasonably certain that the type is Rev. X with the final cinquefoil not showing.

Reverse W.

⚬ INDE : ⚬ ⚬ ⚬   ⚬ ETLIB :

Var. 1. First cinquefoil distant from foot and I. Leaves of branch distant from colon and second cinquefoil. I low, distant from N. L low. B altered from R.

Breaks: Second cinquefoil to branch; from lower part of shields to edge; through second E.   33—W^1

Var. 2. First cinquefoil nearer foot than I. Branch long ending on a level with top of second cinquefoil. Second leaf to left almost touches colon. Left part of date-line triple. Diagonal break across shield. 33^{34}—W^2. 33^{45}—W^2

Var. 3. First cinquefoil and legend distant from milling. Branch ends opposite second cinquefoil. Second and third leaves on left near lower dot of colon. Lower line of E in ET and sloping downward. B low. Lower dot of last colon close to B and shield. 33^{12}—W^3. 33^{25}—W^3. 33^{26}—W^3 33^{44}—W^3

Var. 4. Legend distant from milling. First cinquefoil close to leg of goddess. First colon distant from E and sloping to right. Second leaf on left near colon-dot. Last colon also sloping, the lower dot close to B and cinquefoil. B altered from R.
          44—W^4

Var. 5. Branch-hand opposite space between D and E. N double cut. Break between T and L from pole to milling. 33^{26}—W^5. 44—W^5

Var. 6. INDE widely spaced, I leaning to left. Upper line of first E imperfect. Colon distant from E and still further from cinquefoil, the lower dot below the base line of E. Third cinquefoil relatively high. Second leaf on each side of branch prominent. Branch points to left side of third cinquefoil, ending opposite second. Base of E in ET curved. T high. LIB close at bottom. B a little low. Last colon sloping, the lower dot heavy and entirely on shield. Crack from upper left corner of I to border and from shield to milling. Ryder collection. 33^{10}—W^6

Reverse X.

❋ INDE . ❋ ❋ ❋   ❋ ETLIB . ❋

Var. 1. First cinquefoil near foot, in line with top of I. Fourth cinquefoil low. First colon distant from E and cinquefoil. Last colon close to shield and cinquefoil. Top of branch almost touches third cinquefoil. I low, leaning to left. E in ET low. No curls. $30—X^1$. $32^2—X^1$. $32^7—X^1$

Var. 2. First cinquefoil near foot, its top slightly below the level of top of I. First period near base line of E and partly below it. Last period partly on shield. Last cinquefoil close to shield and opposite the upper curve of B. Branch points a trifle right of the centre of the third cinquefoil. IND widely spaced, with I low and leaning to left. Letters of ETLIB irregular with E high. ET slants to left. IB successively low.

Die-crack connecting the top and bottom of first 7. $32^2—X^2$

Var. 3. First cinquefoil about twice as far from I as from foot. First period touches base line of E. Last period distant from shield, nearer to B than to cinquefoil. Branch points to right of third cinquefoil and ends just below it. E in ET slants to left. Top of T higher than adjoining letters. I in LIB high. B altered from R. $32^1—X^3$

Var. 4. First cinquefoil nearer to foot than to I and partly above the top of I. First period somewhat distant from E and very distant from second cinquefoil. The three cinquefoils between E and head all high. Last period half on shield. Last cinquefoil distant from B and often weakly struck. Letters heavy. Lower line of first E defective. Branch points at third cinquefoil and is distant from it. Second leaf on left points at colon. T high. B low, altered from R. Lower sash-end opposite space between L and I. $32^2—X^4$. $32^3—X^4$

Var. 5. Branch points left of third cinquefoil, its highest point opposite right edge of second. Fourth and fifth cinquefoils low. Last cinquefoil slightly distant from shield. Last colon touches shield. Lower sash-end opposite I. $32^4—X^5$

Var. 6. Branch points at centre of third cinquefoil, ending below it. First period close to E and about half below it. Last period near shield, which is indented opposite the period. Last cinquefoil nearly touches shield. The two lower leaves on each side of branch large and prominent. T in ET and I in LIB slightly high. $32^6—X^6$

Reverse Y.

❋ INDE . ❋ – ❋ – ❋   ❋ ETLIB . ❋

The three cinquefoils after INDE separated by hyphens and widely spaced. Last colon close to B and final cinquefoil. Branch crooked. The lowest leaf on left pointing diagonally downward.   43—Y

Reverse Z.

❋ INDE : ❋ ❋ ❋   ❋ ETLIB : ❋

In varieties 4, 5, 14, 15, 19 and 20 the lower dot of the last colon is distant from the shield.

In varieties 1, 2, 3, 6, 8, 10, 11, 13, 16, 17, 21 and 23 it is close to the shield and touches the shield in var. 12.

In varieties 7, 9, 18 and 24 the lower dot is partly or wholly in the shield.

Var. 1. First cinquefoil close to foot; second, third and fourth nearly equidistant, the third high. Last cinquefoil close to upper dot of colon and shield. First colon low, the lower dot almost all below E. Last colon also low, the dots close, the lower one very near but not touching shield. Top leaf of branch points at right side of third cinquefoil, ending somewhat below it. Branch-hand opposite E. I leans to left. First E struck over an N. E in ET leans to left. Top of T further from E than from L. Lower curve of B too small. Date-line curved over last 7. 8 touches line.

When combined with obv. 33⁴⁰ die-cracks occur from border along the edge of fourth cinquefoil to shoulder and across shield to milling; also from right shoulder to pole-hand.   33¹³—Z¹. 33¹⁹—Z¹. 33³⁸—Z¹. 33⁴⁰—Z¹. 49—Z¹

Var. 2. First cinquefoil nearer to foot than to I. Wider spacing between third and fourth cinquefoils than between second and third. Last cinquefoil near shield and opposite upper colon-dot. Both colons close to letters with the upper dot low. Lower dot of last colon close to shield. Branch-hand opposite E. Leaves distant from colon. Top leaf points to right edge of third cinquefoil, terminating a little below it. Close spacing in INDE. Bottom of LIB close. All figures below date-line. Late issues show vertical break through head and neck.   33⁴—Z². 33¹⁹—Z². 33⁴⁰—Z². 33⁴²—Z²

Var. 3. First cinquefoil high and close to foot. Third cinquefoil nearer to second than to fourth. Last cinquefoil close to colon and shield. Colons regular and near cinquefoils. Branch-hand opposite E. Top leaf points at centre of third cinquefoil and is considerably below it. INDE widely spaced. I in LIB high. B apparently made from an R punch. Figures 1 and last 7 encroach on date-line.

$$32⁴—Z³. \quad 33³³—Z³. \quad 33³⁴—Z³$$

Var. 4. First cinquefoil nearer to foot than to I. The three following cinquefoils nearly equidistant, the second a little low. Last cinquefoil touches shield and is near lower dot of colon. First colon near E and cinquefoil slanting to left, the upper dot low. Last colon near B and a little further from shield. Top leaf points to left part of third cinquefoil and is near to it. E in ET leans to left. LI a trifle high. B connected from R. In date 1 low, 8 touches line, which is curved over both 7's.   33²³—Z⁴

Var. 5. First cinquefoil nearer foot than I. Wider spacing between third and fourth cinquefoils than between second and third. Last cinquefoil distant from shield, opposite space between colon-dots. First colon nearer to E than to cinquefoil, the lower dot opposite second leaf on left of branch. Last colon near B and distant from shield. Branch points to centre of third cinquefoil, the top leaf out of position to the right. I leans to left. All figures of date touch line. Break from D across waist to pole. 33²—Z⁵

Var. 6. First cinquefoil a little nearer to I than to foot. The three following cinquefoils about equidistant. Last cinquefoil close to colon and shield. Colons near cinquefoils. Branch-hand opposite upright of E and space between D and E. Branch long and narrow, printing at centre of third cinquefoil. I low, leaning to left. In ETLIB E and B low. All figures date below line.   33¹³—Z⁶. 33³⁸—Z⁶

Var. 7. First cinquefoil nearer foot than I. Fourth cinquefoil low opposite face. Last cinquefoil high, mostly above upper dot of colon and close to rim of shield. First colon near E distant from cinquefoil. Last colon close to B, slanting to right, the lower dot half on shield. Branch-hand opposite E. Branch wide, its top leaf pointing right of second cinquefoil and terminating opposite the centre of the cinquefoil. First I low, TL widely separated. B low. Date-line defective at left. 1 high, distant from 7. Other figures below line. 33^{10}—Z⁷. 33^{13}—Z⁷. 33^{29}—Z⁷

Var. 8. First cinquefoil nearer foot than I, but distant from both. Following three cinquefoils about equally spaced, the fourth low. Last cinquefoil near shield distant from colon. Lower dot of last colon close to shield and a little nearer B than the upper dot. Branch-hand opposite E and space between D and E. Branch short and broad, pointing nearly at centre of second cinquefoil and terminating well below it. Third leaf on left touches lower dot of colon. In ETLIB E and B low, LI close at bottom. B from an R punch with a long lower line added. Date-line irregular and broken, all figures touching it. 33^{10}—Z⁸

Var. 9. First cinquefoil closer to foot than I, but less distant from I than usual. Third cinquefoil nearer to fourth than to second. Last cinquefoil close to upper dot of colon and touches shield. First colon much nearer to E than to cinquefoil. Upper dot of both colons low. Lower dot of last colon in shield. Branch-hand opposite upright of E and space below. Top of upper leaf about level with right edge of second cinquefoil. N distant from I, its top above that of D. B low, leaning to right. Date-line curved over both 7's. 1 touches the line. 8 encroaches on it. Crack from pole hand through latter part of legend. 33^{20}—Z⁹. 33^{35}—Z⁹. 33^{37}—Z⁹

Var. 10. First cinquefoil near foot. Third cinquefoil nearer to second than to fourth. Last cinquefoil close to shield, distant from colon. Colons distant from letters with the upper dot low. Upper dot of first colon more distant from E. Lower dot of last colon near shield. Branch-hand opposite E. Second leaf on left opposite colon, but distant. Top leaf points at left edge of third cinquefoil and is opposite the highest part of the second. Wide spacing in INDE, the I leaning to left. B slightly low, inclining to right. Lower date-line defective. 33^{7}—Z¹⁰. 33^{24}—Z¹⁰. 33^{25}—Z¹⁰. 44—Z¹⁰

Var. 11. First cinquefoil a little nearer I than foot, but distant from both. The three following cinquefoils equidistant. Last cinquefoil close to shield, distant from colon. Colons distant from letters with upper dot low. Lower dot of last colon near shield. Branch-hand opposite E and space below. Branch points left of third cinquefoil and ends opposite second. Second leaf on left points to lower right corner of E. Lower left corner of second E near pole-hand B altered from R. In date first 7 high, the line above defective. Last 7 low.

Break from milling through upright of T; also from globe through last 7.

33^{20}—Z¹¹. 33^{28}—Z¹¹. 33^{33}—Z¹¹. 33^{34}—Z¹¹. 33^{41}—Z¹¹

Var. 12. First cinquefoil rather far from foot and twice as far from I. Third cinquefoil slightly nearer to fourth than to second. Last cinquefoil close to upper dot of colon and shield. Colons near letters with the upper dot low. Lower dot of last colon close to B and touching shield. Branch-hand opposite space between DE. Branch points left of third cinquefoil and ends slightly above second. Uprights of IB parallel. B low. All figures touch date-line. Die crack from foot to top of first I; through 8; along top of ETLIB. 33^{2}—Z¹²

Var. 13. First cinquefoil about midway between foot and I. Third cinquefoil nearer second than to fourth. Last cinquefoil opposite upper dot of colon and close to shield. Colons close to E and B, the upper dot of both low. Lower dot of last colon near shield. Branch points at left part of third cinquefoil and ends a little above second. Third leaf on left is near colon, pointing to the lower dot. B low. In date 1 high, both 7's below line. Crack through fourth cinquefoil.

$$33^1—Z^{13}. \quad 33^8—Z^{13}. \quad 33^{32}—Z^{13}$$

Var. 14. First cinquefoil low, almost touching figure. The three following cinquefoils equally spaced. Last cinquefoil distant from colon and shield. Both colons low, with their lower dot almost all below the preceding letters. Branch-hand opposite colon and space above it. Branch ends half way between second and third cinquefoils and points just left of the third. Top leaf disconnected to left. I in LIB double cut. 1 touches line, 787 below it. Break from edge nearly to branch between colon and second cinquefoil.

$$33^{14}—Z^{14}$$

Var. 15. First cinquefoil nearly equidistant from foot and I. Much wider spacing between second and third cinquefoils than between third and fourth. Last cinquefoil very close to shield. Colons with dots close. First colon much nearer to E than to cinquefoil. Last colon low, midway between B and cinquefoil, the lower dot rather distant from shield. Branch-hand opposite E and space above it. Branch long, pointing at edge. Fourth leaf from bottom on both sides prominent. First I inclines to left. N high. Top leaf of branch disconnected between second and third cinquefoils. IB low. Lower curve of B double cut. First 7 below, other figures touch date-line. $33^{16}—Z^{15}$

Var. 16. First cinquefoil distant from foot and I. Third cinquefoil slightly nearer second than fourth. Last cinquefoil touches shield, opposite upper dot of colon and distant from it. Upper dot of both colons low. Last colon about twice as far from cinquefoil as from B, the lower dot not far from rim of shield. Branch-hand opposite upright of E and space below. Branch points right of second cinquefoil and ends opposite its lower edge. First I low and distant from N. Upright of T extends below L. B, made with an R punch altered, leans strongly to right. On this reverse the pole-hand is lacking, the arm terminating abruptly below E.

Die-break from milling through top of E. $\quad 33^{12}—Z^{16}. \quad 33^{27}—Z^{16}. \quad 33^{28}—Z^{16}$

Var. 17. First cinquefoil not far from foot, about twice as far from I. Third cinquefoil much nearer to second than to fourth. Last cinquefoil touches shield. Dots of both colons close, the upper dot low. First colon rather near E, very distant from cinquefoil. Last colon slopes to left, the lower dot very close to shield. Branch-hand mostly opposite space between E and colon. Branch points at left part of third cinquefoil ending just above second. Second leaf from top on left near cinquefoil. Top of letters in INDE not all on same curve. ET wide. LI close at base. Date line defective over both 7's.

Long break through E across figure to border. Break at right of foot through date line. $\quad 33^2—Z^{17}$

Var. 18. First cinquefoil near foot and low. Widest spacing between second and third cinquefoils. Last cinquefoil close to upper dot of colon and touches shield. Lower dot of last colon half on shield. Branch-hand opposite E. Branch points at left part

of third cinquefoil, its top between second and third. LI close at base. Lower curve of
B close to shield. Date-line curved over 1 and both 7's. 33^{11}—Z^{18}

Var. 19. First cinquefoil about equidistant from foot and I. Three following
cinquefoils equally spaced. Last cinquefoil distant from shield, opposite space between
dots of colon. Last colon midway between B and cinquefoil and distant from shield.
Branch-hand opposite E and space below it. Branch points at left edge of third cinquefoil, the top leaf a little above second. Second leaf on left very near colon. First E
high, leaning to right. Lower corner of E in ET distant from pole-hand. Lower curve
of B small. Date about evenly spaced. 33^1—Z^{19}. 33^8—Z^{19}

Var. 20. First cinquefoil high, distant from foot and I. Group of three cinquefoils about equally spaced. Last cinquefoil rather distant from shield. Dots of first
colon close, the upper are low. Last colon midway between B and cinquefoil, the lower
dot distant from shield. Branch-hand opposite space between D and E. Top of branch
opposite second cinquefoil, pointing to left of third. D low. Top of first E leans to right.
Last 7 low.

Heavy break over last cinquefoil, extending later to upper part of B. Semi-circular
figures encroach on date-line. 33^2—Z^{21}. 33^{12}—Z^{21}

Var. 21. First cinquefoil high, a little nearer to foot than to I. Group of three
cinquefoils widely and evenly spaced. Last cinquefoil near upper dot of colon and
shield. First colon sloping, the lower dot nearer E. Last colon also sloping, the dots
close, the lower one very near shield. Branch-hand opposite right part of E and space
between E and colon. Branch points at third cinquefoil, the top leaf a little below it.
Top of N above that of D. N struck with a punch altered probably from an O. All
figures encroach on date-line. 33^2—Z^{21}. 38^{12}—Z^{21}

Var. 22. First cinquefoil high, nearer foot than I. Second and third cinquefoils
more widely spaced than third and fourth. Last cinquefoil very near or touching upper
dot of colon. Branch short, pointing between second and third cinquefoils. Top leaf
about opposite right edge of second cinquefoil. Branch-hand opposite E. N struck with
same altered punch as in Z^{21}.

Heavy break near milling to right of fourth cinquefoil. 33^2—Z^{22}

Var. 23. First cinquefoil distant from foot and I. The following group of three
evenly and rather closely spaced. Last cinquefoil close to shield. First colon distant
from E and still more so from cinquefoil. Last colon nearer to cinquefoil than to B,
the lower dot very close to shield. Branch-hand opposite space between D and E. Top
leaf disconnected and pointing at third cinquefoil. B low leaning to right.

Heavy break from shoulder to milling between third and fourth cinquefoils. Die
crack from edge through lower right corner of L. 33^{38}—Z^{23}

Var. 24. First cinquefoil high in line with top of I. Group of three cinquefoils
about evenly spaced. Last cinquefoil distant from upper dot of colon and close to shield.
First colon slants to right and is distant from cinquefoil. Last colon very low, the lower
dot entirely on shield. Branch-hand opposite E. Branch points to third cinquefoil,
ending about half way between second and third. First I low and double cut. N high.
LIB successively low. B altered from R. Figure 1 small, leaning to left. In some speci-

mens a heavy break occurs from milling above fourth cinquefoil extending downward across shoulder and drapery to the milling on the right of 7. This break is especially noticeable when reverse 24 is combined with obverse 18.

$$33^{12}—Z^{24}. \quad 33^{18}—Z^{24}. \quad 33^{25}—Z^{38}$$

Reverse a.

× INDE : – + — + –   – + – ETLIB :

Var. 1. Large letters. Branch-hand opposite E. Third leaf on left of branch close to lower dot of colon. L high. Lower line of B light. Lower dot of last colon on shield. Break from upper right corner of L to edge.   26—a^1. 27—a^1

Var. 2. Large letters. Branch-hand opposite D. Top leaf near lower dot of colon. E in ET low. Left lower corner of T defective. Last colon very low. Upper dot touches rim, lower dot all on shield.   20—a^2. 29—a^2

Var. 3. Large letters. Branch-hand opposite upright of E. Branch points at second cross. IB successively low. Hyphen to left of fourth cross on hair. Hyphen to right of fourth cross touches pole. 78 widely spaced.   47—a^3

Reverse b.

× INDE : – + – – + –   + – ETLIB :

Letters large. Branch-hand opposite upright of E and space between D and E. Left lower corner of E in ET distant from pole-hand. B well clear of shield. Last colon low, the lower dot nearly all on shield.   25—b

Reverse c.

+ –INDE : – + – – + –   – + – ETLIB :

Crosby describes this die in combination with obv. 22. Hall did not succeed in finding it and authentic examples are lacking.

Reverse d.

* INDE : +   + ETLIB :

Another die listed on Crosby's authority, but lacking later confirmation. Crosby combines it with obv. 26.

Reverse e.

+ INDE : ·◄·◄·   + ETLIB :

Branch-hand opposite D. Top leaf points at large dot of ornament. Wide spacing between TL. B distant from shield. Last colon low, the lower dot part on shield.   37^5—e. 37^9—e

Reverse f.

– + –INDE : + +   – + – ET – LIB :

Crosby describes this die as reverse F of the draped busts of 1787 and combines it with obv. 24. We have met no specimens that exactly conform to it. Reverse FF is similar, but without hyphens to 4th cross.

Reverse g.

−✛−INDE : − ✛− − ✛−   − ✛− ET − LIB :

Var. 1. Letters small. Branch-hand opposite upright of E and space between D and E. Top leaf near second cross. Hyphen to right of third cross very distant from head. Hyphen to right of fourth cross near pole. Upper dot of both colons low. Lower dot of last colon half on shield. Liberty pole touches date-line midway between 1 and 7. $18-g^1$

Var. 2. Letters small. Branch-hand opposite E and space between D and E. Top of branch about level with right extremity of second cross. Lower line of L long. Pole touches date-line just above the left upper corner of first 7. Lower dot of last colon partly on shield. $22-g^2$

Var. 3. Letters small. Branch-hand opposite D. Top leaf of branch near hyphen to left of second cross. Hyphen to right of fourth cross joins the cross. A line unites the hyphen in ET—LIB with the right top of T. Lower dot of last colon very close to shield. I touches date line, other figures below it. $17-g^3$. $24-g^3$

Var. 4. Letters small. Branch-hand opposite right part of D. Top leaf points at left edge of second cross and is close to it. Hyphen to left of first cross touches figure just above the foot. Hyphen to left joins third cross. Hyphen to right of fourth cross touches pole and looks like a projecting finger. Lower dot of last colon touches shield. Upper date line the longer. Break below IN. Crack along bottom of date.

$19-g^4$

Var. 5. Letters small. Branch-hand opposite D and space between D and E. Top of upper left touches colon-dot. Hyphen to right of first cross weak. Hyphen to left of fourth cross below plume. Last colon clear of shield. Light break from upper left corner of first E. $24-g^5$. $48-g^5$

Reverse h.

✛ INDE : ⬤⬤   ✖ ET − LIB :

Var. 1. Branch-hand opposite D. Top of branch level with right edge of first colon, IN widely spaced. Lower curve of B light. 39^1-h^1

Var. 2. Top of branch near large dot of ornament. Letters in INDE about evenly spaced. 37^7-h^2

Reverse i.

✛ INDE : ⬤⬤   // ET − LIB : ✖

Branch-hand opposite E. Branch points to large dot of ornament. Scroll nearly or quite touches head. Base line of I in LIB long. 37^3-i

Reverse k.

// INDE : ⬤⬤   // ET − LIB :

The legend of k is the same as that of reverse cc, except the final letter, which in reverse cc is an R.

Var. 1. Branch-hand opposite space between D and E. Top of branch opposite middle of space between colon and ornament. Foliage scanty. First scroll near foot of goddess. 37^4-k^1

Var. 2. Branch-hand opposite D and space between D and E. Upper leaf of branch partly on large dot of ornament. Period-like dot in field below the smaller fleuron of ornament. Last colon low, sloping to right, the lower dot almost all below B. 37^8—k^2

Var. 3. Upper leaf ends opposite centre of large dot. First scroll very near or touching goddess. Lower edge of last colon on same curve as bottom of adjacent B.

34—K^3 36—k^3

Var. 4. Top leaf unusually large and almost touching large dot. Right lower corner of B square and heavy, apparently altered from R. Last 7 low. Die broken on edge above ornament. 37^6—k^4

Var. 5. Branch-hand opposite upright of D and space between N and D. Branch ends opposite space between E and colon. No terminal leaf. Second leaf on right large and prominent. Second scroll almost touches head. 37^2—k^5

Reverse l.

◄◄ INDE : ►◄◄►-   **◄◄ ET – LIB : ◄**

Var. 1. Branch-hand opposite D. Top of branch just beyond first colon. B altered from R. Last fleuron touches shield. I high. Last 7 below line. 36—l^1

Var. 2. Branch-hand opposite space between D and E. Branch short and wide, pointing to large dot of ornament. B altered from R. Both 7's below date-line.

16^3—l^2. 33^{16}—l^2. 38—l^2

Reverse m.

✶ INDE ✶ ✶   **✶ ET – LIB ✶**

Large letters. Branch points to second star. Last star distant from B and close to shield. Stars with five blunt points. Wide date. 16^1--m. 25—m. 28--m

Reverse n.

✶ INDE : ✶ ✶   **✶ ET – LIB :**

Branch-hand opposite upright of D and space between N and D. Branch nearly or quite touches lower dot of colon. INDE and ET widely spaced. LIB rather close. Colon dots heavy. Lower dot of last colon touches shield. 16^4—n. 16^5—n. 28—n. 29—n

Reverse o.

✶ INDE ✶ ✶   **ETLIB ✶**

Branch-hand opposite D. Branch points at second star. Top leaf disconnected. INDE widely spaced. Letters large. LIB successively low.

Break through lower part of second E, also from left upper corner of L.

28—o. 29^2—o. 42—o

Reverse p.

✶ INDE ✶ ✶   **✶ ETLIB ✶**

First star close to foot. Last star touches shield and is usually weak. Specimens occur in which only faint traces of the star are found. ND widely spaced. LI very close at bottom. 16^5—p 29^1—p

Reverse q.

INDE : ❖ ❖ ❖   ❖ ETLIB : ❖

Top leaf of branch disconnected to right. A line connects the corners of first E. IB successively low and close at bottom. Lower dot of last colon imperfect and touches shield.

Curved breaks from head to pole, and from pole-hand to cinquefoil and milling.

$$33^4—q \quad 33^{13}—q \quad 33^{19}—q \quad 33^{43}—q$$

Reverse r.

❖ INDE : ❖ ❖   ❖ ET LIB :

Var. 1. Branch-hand opposite E. Branch points right of second cinquefoil. Third leaf on left disconnected. Bottom of L high, top leans to left. B struck over a cinquefoil. Lower dot of last colon close to, but clear of shield. In date 1 slants to left and is distant from 7. $33^{15}—r^1 \quad 33^{17}—r^1$

Var. 2. Branch-hand opposite upright of E and space between D and E. Branch points right of second cinquefoil. Third leaf on right disconnected. B over a cinquefoil. Dots of colon close and heavy. Last colon sloping, the lower dot very close to B. Late impression show the B slightly open below. $33^7—r^2$

Var. 3. Branch-hand opposite upright of E and space between D and E. Branch points at left edge of second cinquefoil. No additional spacing between ET and LIB. Upper dot of last colon low, the lower dot close to but clear of shield. In date 1 and first 7 encroach on date-line. Break along top of NDE to second cinquefoil; also from lower left corner of I. $31^2—r^3$

Var. 4. Branch-hand opposite E. Branch points at centre of second cinquefoil. IB close at bottom. Dots of last colon touch each other, the lower dot half on shield.

$$31^1—r^4 \quad 33^7—r^4 \quad 33^{27}—r^4$$

Var. 5. Branch-hand opposite space between D and E. Branch points at centre of second cinquefoil and terminates near it. Third leaf on left close to colon-dot. Fourth cinquefoil nearer pole than head. Lower line of B prolonged to left of upright. B over a cinquefoil. Lower dot of last colon mostly below B and well clear of shield. Lower date-line lighter than upper and not continuous.

Die-crack through second, third and fourth cinquefoils to pole; another from knee of goddess through right side of first cinquefoil.

This very rare reverse is not found in Hall's printed list. In his later notes he records finding a specimen after twenty years search. $33^{17}—r^5$

Reverse s.

❖ INDE : ❖ ❖   ❖ ET – LIB : ❖

Var. 1. Branch ends a little above second cinquefoil and points at border. First I low. E in ET leans to left. Second leaf on right of branch long.

Break from milling to front of head. Crack from milling through third cinquefoil.

$$33^{39}—s^1$$

Var. 2. Branch ends above second cinquefoil and points to border. Second leaf on left long. E in ET slightly high, the top leaning to left. Lower dot of last colon nearly all below B. First 7 of date encroaches on date-line.

Break from upper left corner of I. 33^9—s^2

Reverse u.

⊛ INDE ⊛ ⊛   ⊛ ETLIB

Apparently re-cut from the die of reverse p, the stars having the appearance of trefoils. Letters all badly formed and double cut. Arm holding branch consists of two parallel lines. Date weaker than in reverse p and date-lines further apart.

Only one specimen known. 16^5—u

Reverse aa.

⊛ FNDE . ⊛ ⊛ ⊛   ⊛ ETLIB . ⊛

F punch used instead of I for first letter of legend. N double cut. Lower line of both E's long. Right arm of T too long, reaching nearly to top of L. In ETLIB T and I high. 32^5—aa. 32^8—aa

Reverse bb

✗ INDE : − + − − + −   − + − ETLIR :

Crosby gives this reverse in the combination $26^?$—B. With exception of the final R instead of B the legend is the same as reverse a. In some cases it is difficult to determine whether the final letter should be described as B or R. As well defined examples of this reverse do not seem to occur, it is probably a duplication of reverse a.

Reverse cc.

ƒƒ INDE : ⤆⤆⤆   ƒƒ ET-LIR :

Legend the same as reverse k, except final letter.

Var. 1. Branch-hand opposite D and space between D and E. Top leaf points at large dot of ornament. First scroll clear of goddess. IR successively low. The final R looks somewhat like an open B, the tail not curving to right. 37^1—cc^1

Var. 2. Branch-hand entirely opposite D. Top leaf points to large dot and terminates a little above the colon. ET on higher plane than LIR. R like open B. Lower dot of last colon all below R. 37^{14}—cc^2

Reverse dd.

⤜ INDE : ⤆⤆⤆   ⤜ ET-LIR : ⤜

Crosby combines this reverse—his D—with obverse 37. The legend is identical with reverse HH except the final letter. Compare remark under reverse bb.

Reverse ee.

⤜ INDE : ⤆⤆⤆   ⤜ ET-LIR :

Branch-hand opposite D and space between D and E. Top leaf points to large dot and terminates near it. Lower dot of last colon between tail of R and shield, and close to both. 39^2—ee

Reverse ff.

<< INDE : <•>•   << ET-LIR : •

Legend same as reverse l, except final letter.

Var. 1. Top of highest leaf above right edge of colon. Index finger of pole-hand long and prominent. Second E touches pole-hand. Tail of R sharp. Lower dot of last colon mostly below R. Lower date-line broken above figure 1. 33^{13}—ff^1.   34—ff^1

Var. 2. Top of highest leaf opposite right edge of first colon. Fleurons right of head nearly unite. E distant from pole-hand. In ETLIR T high and R low. Last fleuron touches shield.   36—ff^2 37^{11}—ff^2 39^1—ff^2

Reverse gg.

• INDE : • •   • ETLIR : •

Legend same as in reverse T except final letter.

Var. 1. First cinquefoil high. Lower dot of first colon near prominent leaf on left of branch. Last cinquefoil touches shield.

Break from fourth cinquefoil to milling. In some combinations there is a break from waist to D and thence to left to N. 31^1—gg^1 33^{11}—gg^1 33^{20}—gg^1 33^{38}—gg^1

Var. 2. Leaves of branch distant from first colon. T high. Last cinquefoil well separated from shield.

Break from shield through last cinquefoil and above IR to milling.

     33^{17}—gg^2. 33^{31}—gg^2

Reverse hh.

• INDE : • • •   • ETLIR : •

Legend the same as in reverse Z except final R instead of B.

Var. 1. The three cinquefoils after INDE about equidistant. Last cinquefoil partly on shield. Tail of R sharp and close to lower dot of colon. Last colon very low, the lower dot part on shield.

Die-cracks from foot along top of IND; from milling across shield; from date line through date.   30—hh^1

Var. 2. Wider spacing between third and fourth cinquefoils than between second and third. Last colon and last cinquefoil clear of shield. Base line of first E touches lower dot of colon. Tail of R short. All figures below line.

     33^{13}—hh^2. 33^{23}—hh^2. 33^{43}—hh^2

Reverse ii.

• INDE : • •   • ETIIB :

Leaves of branch irregular. Nine on left side opposite colon. A short line extends to left from top leaf. Last colon weak, the lower dot partly on shield.

A slight crack from bottom of first I in IIB to upper sash-end.   41—ii

Reverse kk.

• INDE :• •   • ETIIB : •

Var. 1. Branch-hand mostly opposite space between D and E. Lower dot of last colon partly on shield. Last star distance from colon.   26—kk^1.   40—kk^1

Var. 2. Branch-hand opposite E. Lower dot of last colon well separated from shield. Last star near colon.   42—kk²

Reverse AA.

✸ INDE : ✚ ─✚   ✚ ETLIB :

Letters large. Branch-hand opposite upright of E. Branch points between the arms of second cross. Hyphen to right touches third cross. TL close at top. B partly on shield. Lower dot of last colon entirely on shield. Pointed end of upper sash opposite upright of T.   26—AA

Reverse BB.

✖ INDE : ✚ ─✚─   ✚ ETLIB ·

Letters large. Branch points at lowest part of second cross. Branch hand opposite right part of E. B partly on shield. Period close to shield.   46—BB

Reverse CC.

✚ INDE : ─✳─ ✳─   ─✚─ ET LIB :

Letters small. Top of branch opposite centre of first colon. Last colon clear of shield. Last 7 below date-line.   45—CC

Reverse DD.

─✚─INDE : ✚ ─✚─   ─✚─ ET-LIB :

Hyphen to left of first cross distant from goddess, the one to right touches the cross. Hyphen between ET and LIB joins the right top of T. Branch-hand opposite space between D and E. Top leaf points to second cross and is close to it. Lower dot of last colon touches shield. All figures touch date-line.   21—DD

Reverse EE.

✦ INDE : ✦─✦─   ─✦ ET-LIB :✦

Branch-hand opposite right part of D and space beyond it. Top of branch touches lower dot of first colon. Cinquefoils rather distant from colons. D low. 33³⁰—EE

Reverse FF.

─✚─INDE : ✚ ✚   ✚ ET-LIB :

Letters small. Branch-hand opposite D. Top of upper leaf opposite centre of colon. Lower dot of last colon clear of shield. 1 and both 7's below date line. Slight break from E in ET to edge.   24—FF. 53—FF

Reverse GG.

─✚─INDE : ─✚═✚─   ─✚─ ET-LIB :

Letters small. Branch-hand opposite D and space between ND. Branch has twelve leaves arranged in triplets. Top leaf points at lower dot of first colon. Two hyphens between second and third cross, the upper one sometimes weak. Hyphen to right joins fourth cross. Wide spacing in IND.   38—GG

Reverse HH.

✦✦ INDE : ✦✦✦   ✦ ET-LIB : ✦

Legend the same as dd except final letter.
Branch-hand opposite space between ND. Top leaf very close to lower right corner of E. Hyphen in ET-LIB short. Lower line of B weak, in most specimens making the

B look like R. This circumstance doubtless explains Crosby's reverse *D,* which has been retained in this list as dd. Unless some other difference should be discovered in the dies the reverse dd should be eliminated. 37^{13}—HH 37^{8}—HH

Reverse II.

✦ INDE ✦ ✦ ✦   ✦ ETLIB ✦

Legend has six cinquefoils without other punctuation. INDE widely spaced. Letters in ETLIB irregular, the E and B low. B from altered R punch. Date-line triple.

Break from milling between third and fourth cinquefoils.

33^{22}—II. Ryder Collection. Unique

Reverse KK.

✦ INDE : ✦ ✦ ✦   ET LIB : ✦

First E altered from an F. Lower part of L imperfect, probably altered from an I. First colon inclines to right, the dots large and well spaced. Figure 1 low leaning to left. Lower date-line defective. 33^{6}—KK

Reverse LL.

✦ INDE : ✦ ✦   ✦ ET · I IB : ✦

Stars with blunt rays. Upper leaf on left of branch close to colon. Wide spacing between II. Corner of E touches pole-hand. A short line just right of the space between the dots of the first colon. 37^{8}—LL. 37^{12}—LL

Reverse NN.

✦ INDE : ✦ ✦   ✦ ET · LIB :

Stars with blunt rays. Legend similar to reverse N, except period substituted for hyphen in ET.LIB.

Var. 1. Branch points left of second star. Second leaf on left points at lower left corner of E. Top of E in ET above top of T. Last colon slopes to right, the lower dot small and near shield. The date-lines heavy and merging together at both ends.

16^{2}—NN^{1}

Var. 2. Branch points at centre of second star. Third leaf on left points at upright of E. Top of E in ET about in line with top of T. LIB low. Lower dot of last colon more distant from shield than in Var. 1. Date-line quadruple, the lowest line light and running through the tops of the figures. Small 8 in date. 16^{6}—NN^{2}

Reverse RR

➤✦ INDE : ✦✦✦✦   ➤✦ ET-LIB : ✦

Branch-hand opposite space between D and E. Top leaf points at centre of large dot. B low and apparently altered from R. Tip of last fleuron touches shield. In date 1 high, last 7 low. 37^{7}—RR. 37^{10}—RR

Reverse SS

✦ INDE : ✦ ·✦· —   — ✦ ET · LIB : ✦

Cinquefoils heavy. Top leaf points at lower dot of first colon. Lower left corner of E in ET above opposite wrist of pole-arm. First I high, leaning to left. T high. Last 7 below date-line. 33^{30}—SS. 33^{36}—SS

Reverse TT.

— ❀ —INDE : ❀ ❀   — ❀ —   ETLIB : ❀

Dr. Hall describes this reverse as follows: "Specimens examined four. Traces of other hyphens. Bottoms of I and N in same curve. Wide spacing in IND. Branch points at lower period of first colon. Branch-hand opposite upright of D and space between N and D. Hyphen to right connects with fourth cinquefoil. Cinquefoils heavy."

37¹²—TT

Reverse VV.

INDE   ETLIB •

Branch-hand opposite lower right corner of E. From Dr. Hall's later notes.

1¹—VV

Reverse WW.

ET LIB   INDE •

Liberty reversed, holding staff with Liberty Cap in right hand, branch in left. Dr. Hall's later notes.

1⁴—WW

1788 — OBVERSE

Obverses 1 to 6 inclusive have mailed busts facing right.
Obverses 7 to 13 inclusive have mailed busts facing left.
Obverses 14 to 17 inclusive have draped busts.

Obverse 1.

AUCTORI   CONNEC

Smallest head of the year. Same as obv. 1 of 1787.   1—I (R⁶)

Obverse 2.

❀ AUCTORI •   CONNEC ❀

Stars with five sharp points. Period distant from I. Break connects first star with foot of A. Later breaks from lower left corner of mail to border, from top of wreath to border and from last star to milling.   2—Ɖ (R²)

Obverse 3.

❀ AUCTORI ❀   ❀ CONNEC ❀

Var. 1. Stars with six points. First star double cut.   Top of wreath projects considerably above head. Last star near mail.   3¹—B¹ (R⁵)

Var. 2. Similar to Var. 1 but no double cutting of first star.   3²—B² (R⁵)

Obverse 4.

AUCTORI ❀   ❀ CONNEC ❀

Var. 1. Stars with six points. First star over head. Second star near top leaf of wreath. CONNEC widely spaced.   4¹—B¹ (R⁵). 4¹—K. (R⁴)

Var. 2. Second star about midway between top leaf of wreath and C. First C in CONNEC low.   4²—R (R⁶)

Obverse 5.

✳ AUCTORI ✳   ✳ CONNEC ♣

Stars with six points. First star close to both mail and A. Tail of R joins base of I. NN widely spaced.   5—B² (R⁵)

Obverse 6.

AUCTORI ✳   ✳ CONNEC ✳

Stars with six points. Stars distant from letters. Tail of R heavy and well separated from base of I. Break or imperfection in die, connecting lips with chin. A rare variety seldom obtainable in good condition.   6—H (R⁶)

Obverse 7.

✳ AUCTORI. ✳   ✳ CONNEC ✳

In this and the five following obverses the mailed bust faces left. Stars with five blind points. First and last stars touch mail. Twelve leaves in triplets. A slopes to left. NN wide. Curved break from lowest curl. 7—E (R⁴). 7—F (R⁶). 7—K (R⁵)

Obverse 8.

AUCTORI. ✿   CONNEC ✿

Twelve leaves in triplets. Period after I close to forehead. Defect, resembling a misplaced period, on the lower curve of final C. CONNEC weak, the die showing injury. Same die as obv. 12 of 1787.   8—K. (R⁵)

Obverse 9.

AUCTORI .   CONNEC ✳

Star with six sharp points. Wreath with seven outlined leaves. Some specimens show tops of two 8's incused above head near upper leaf. Coarse, serrated milling.

9—E. (R⁴)

Obverse 10.

AUCTORI ✳   ✳ CONNEC ✳

Stars with six points. In obverse 6 which has the same legend the bust faces right and the features and style of bust are quite different.   10—C. (R⁵)

Obverse 11.

✳ AUCTORI   ✳ CONNEC ✳

Stars with six points. First star near A. Point of second star barely touches head. Last star distant from C and mail.   11—G (R²)

Obverse 12.

✳ AUCTORI ✳   ✳ CONNEC ✳

Same punctuation as in Obv. 7 except that stars have six instead of five points.

Var. 1. First star midway between A and mail. Third star partly in head. Three berries in wreath. Short line from lower fillet-end. When connected with Rev. E this die is generally found badly shattered on the head and in both fields.

12¹—E(R³). 12¹—F (R³)

Var. 2. First star near A.   Third star clear of head.   No berries in wreath.

12²—C (R³).   12²—E (R³)

Obverse 13.

❧ AUCTORI ❧   ❧ CONNLC ❧

AU widely spaced.   Last C large and low.   Last cinquefoil distant from C.

13—A¹ (R⁴)

Obverse 14.

❧ AUCTORI ❧   ❧ CONNEC ❧

Draped bust facing left.

Var. 1. First cinquefoil near point of bust, its upper edge about in line with the top of A.   Second cinquefoil to left of hair.   Last cinquefoil connects C with toga.   Most letters closely spaced.   C touches head.   14¹—L² (R⁴)

Var. 2. First cinquefoil opposite middle of A.   Second cinquefoil entirely above hair.   Last cinquefoil between the ends of the toga.   Legend widely spaced.   C in CONNEC clear of head.   14²—A² (R⁴)

Obverse 15.

❧ AUCTORI ❧   ❧ CONNEC. ❧

Draped bust facing left.

Var. 1. Third cinquefoil close to head and much nearer to C than to wreath.   Last cinquefoil between ends of toga.   Lower fillet-end points to period, which is a little nearer C than toga.   Scratches in die extending downward from tail of R and base of I.   Break from nose along left edge of O.   15¹—L¹ (R⁴)

Var. 2. Third cinquefoil rather nearer to wreath than to C.   Last cinquefoil partly above end of toga and midway between period and toga.   Period opposite upper fillet-end.   Break from milling touching final C.   15²—P (R⁴)

Var. 3. First cinquefoil high, nearly half under and distant from bust.   A small and low.   CT wide.   C very close to head, O more distant.   EC close.   Break from milling through left part of final C as in 15².   Only known specimen in poor condition.   Canfield collection.   15³—P (R⁶)

Obverse 16.

❧ AUCTORI. ❧   ❧ CONNEC. ❧

Draped bust facing left.

Var. 1. First cinquefoil high, partly under bust.   Second cinquefoil distant from period and hair.   Third cinquefoil nearer C than wreath.   Last cinquefoil near end of toga and partly above it.   Last period below fillet-ends.   O in CONNEC distant from head.   CO rather widely spaced.

Good specimens show an additional cinquefoil, probably accidental, within the drapery near the centre of its lower edge.   16¹—D (R²).   16¹—H (R²)

Var. 2. Cinquefoil large.   First low, entirely left of bust.   Second and third near wreath.   Last cinquefoil high, partly above end of toga.   Last period opposite upper fillet-end and mostly below C.   C clear of head, O rather distant.   NN widely spaced.

16²—O (R⁴)

Var. 3. First cinquefoil high, about half under bust. Second distant from hair, partly above it. Third nearer c than wreath. Last cinquefoil distant from toga, close to border. First period partly below ɪ. Upper fillet-end points to last period. First c large and high. AUC more widely spaced than following letters. c partly on head, o close, leaning to left. Break from toga to a point near lower fillet-end.   16³—N (R²)

Var. 4. First cinquefoil a trifle high, entirely left of bust. Second distant to left of wreath. Third high, distant from c and wreath. Last cinquefoil nearer colon than toga. Both periods below letters. c touches head, o rather distant from head and c.
16⁴—L² (R⁴)

Var. 5. Letters small and light. First cinquefoil about half under and touching bust. RI more widely spaced than other letters of AUCTORI. First period small and distant from base of ɪ. Third cinquefoil much nearer c than wreath. c just touches head, o not so close as in 16⁶, but closer than in 16¹. Letters in CONNEC irregular, the first N high, the c low. Lower fillet-end points at last cinquefoil.   16⁵—H (R⁴)

Var. 6. The die of 16⁵ recut. Letters much heavier, the ɪ especially thick and badly shaped. R and ɪ closer than in 16⁵. First period close to base of ɪ. Last period close to final cinquefoil. Lower part of c on head, o very close. Lower fillet-end opposite last colon.   16⁶—H (R⁵)

Obverse 17.

⚹ AUCTORI. ⚹   ⚹ CONNLC. ⚹

Draped bust facing left. First cinquefoil entirely left of bust and rather near A. Last cinquefoil between ends of toga. Both fillet-ends opposite final c. First c in CONNEC clear of head. Final c low. Last period below fillet-ends and close to end of toga.   17—O (R⁵). 17—Q (R⁵)

1788 — REVERSE

Reverse A.

⚹ INDE ⚹ ET ⚹   ⚹   ⚹ LIB ⚹

Var. 1. D large and extending above the other letters in INDE. Leaves of branch crude. No top leaf. A small twig from top of stem points to lower right corner of E. ET close.

Break downward from knee touching ɪ and first cinquefoil.   13—A¹

Var. 2. Bottom of D below that of E. Leaves better formed. Top leaf just below the middle of the base line of E. ET and LIB widely spaced. In date 78 low. 14²—A²

Reverse B.

INDE ⚹ ET   LIB ⚹

Var. 1. Star after INDE low. Branch-hand opposite right part of E. Second leaf on left points to the star. In date both 8's slant to right. Heavy serrated milling.
3¹—B¹. 4¹—B¹

Var. 2. D wide. Branch-hand opposite E. Second leaf on left points to lower right corner of E in INDE. In date 1 distant from 7.   3²—B². 5—B²

Reverse C.

INDE ✶ ET   LIB ✶

Branch-hand opposite right part of D and space between D and E. Top of branch points to right of first star. 1 and last 8 encroach on date-line.

Break from last cinquefoil downward to edge opposite lower part of shield.

10—C. 12²—C

Reverse D.

INDE ✶ ET ✶   LIB ✶

Branch-hand points at first star. Top of branch points at base of T.

Breaks at E in ET, and I in LIB. Also later at foot of Liberty and from B to shield.

2—D. 16¹—D

Reverse E.

INDE ✶ ET ✶   ✶ LIB ✦

Branch-hand opposite E. Branch points to lower left corner of E in ET. Branch curve of shield and from last cinquefoil to milling. 6—H. 16¹—H, 16⁵—H, 16⁶—H

Reverse F.

INDE ✶ ET ✶   ✶   LIB ✶

First star near E in ET. Third star between head and pole. Last star low. Branch points at edge of first star. A line parallel to the upright joins the left corners of B.

7—F. 12¹—F

Reverse G.

INDE ✶ ET ✶   ✶ LIB ✶

Branch-hand opposite space between D and E. Branch short pointing to edge of star. Third star between pole-hand and L. Both 8's slope to right.   11—G

Reverse H.

✦ INDE. ✦ ✦   ✦ ETLIB. ✦

Branch-hand opposite D. Branch points at first period. Fourth cinquefoil between head and pole. INDE widely spaced. ETL close. 7 low. Die-cracks occur from D to a point below knee of goddess, thence downward to edge; along top of ETL; through lower narrow with small leaves. Coarse milling.   7—E. 9—E. 12¹—E. 12²—E

Reverse I.

INDE ×   ET · LIB ×

TL widely spaced. Same die as Crosby's reverse B of the Vermont cent of 1788.

1—I

Reverse K.

✶ INDE ✶   ET ✶ LIB ✶

First star much nearer to I than to foot. Star between T and L close to both letters. First I imperfect at top. Branch ends opposite right corner of E. 4¹—K. 7—K. 8—K

Reverse L.

⚜ INDE • ET ⚜   ⚜   LIB. ⚜

Var. 1. First cinquefoil near foot; third between head and pole; last close to lower part of shield. Branch broad. Top leaf opposite middle of upright of E in ET. Two bow-strings below hair puff. LIB wide. 15^1—L^1

Var. 2. First cinquefoil about equidistant from foot and I. Second cinquefoil low, opposite face. Top leaf near upper left corner of E in ET. One leaf on right touches lower left corner of same E. E low in INDE, high in ET. Last period distant from B. 78 low. No bow-strings. 14^1—L^2. 16^4—L^2

Reverse M.

INDE • ET ⚜   ⚜ ⚜ LIB. ⚜

Crosby gives this reverse combined with Obv. 15. Have met with no specimens.

Reverse N.

⚜ IN DE. ⚜ ⚜   ⚜ ⚜ ETLIB. ⚜

Branch-hand opposite D and space to left. Top leaf points at first period. Last period half on shield. 8's high and widely spaced.

Occasional specimens are found on large planchets, the dies showing wear. On these pieces the periods are elongated and the lettering fine and irregular. The pole-hand and parts of the date-line are lacking. 16^3—N

Reverse O.

⚜ INDL. ET ⚜ ⚜   ⚜ ⚜ LIB. ⚜

Branch-hand mostly opposite space between L and period. Top leaf ends between E and T. Last cinquefoil distant from period and shield. Bow-strings below hair-puff. Pole has Liberty cap. 16^2—O. 17—O

Reverse P.

⚜ INDE • ET ⚜ ⚜   ⚜ ⚜ LIB. ⚜

Branch-hand opposite period. Top-leaf points at T. Last cinquefoil distant from period and near shield. 15^2—P. 15^3—P

Reverse Q.

⚜ INDE • ET ⚜   ⚜ ⚜ LIB. ⚜

Branch-hand opposite space between E and period. Two bow-strings below hair-puff. A plume curves downward and backward from top of hair-puff.

Irregular break from lower right corner of E in INDE to first cinquefoil.   17—Q

Reverse R.

✕ INDE ✱ ✱ ET   ✱ LIB ✱

Top of upper leaf of branch about opposite lower right corner of D. Specimens too poor for better description. 4^2—R

LIST OF VARIETIES AND COMBINATIONS.

1785

Obv.	Rev.	Rarity	Obv.	Rev.	Rarity	Obv.	Rev.	Rarity
1	E	R^4	3^5	K^2	R^5	6^2	F^1	R^4
2	A^1	R^3	4^1	F^4	R^1	6^3	G^1	R^3
2	A^4	R^3	4^2	F^4	R^6	6^3	G^2	R^4
3^1	A^3	R^3	4^3	A^2	R^3	6^4	F^5	R^5
3^1	L	R^4	4^3	D	R^4	6^4	I	R^3
3^2	L	R^3	4^4	C	R^4	6^4	K^1	R^5
3^3	F^3	R^4	4^4	D	R^4	6^5	M	R^5
3^4	F^1	R^3	5^1	F^5	R^4	7	D	R^5
3^4	F^2	R^3	5^2	F^5	R^4	8	D	R^6
3^5	B	R^2	6^1	A^1	R^3			

1786

Obv.	Rev.	Rarity	Obv.	Rev.	Rarity	Obv.	Rev.	Rarity
1	A	R^4	5^3	B^2	R^6	5^8	O^2	R^3
2^1	A	R^3	5^3	G	R^5	5^9	B^1	R^4
2^1	D^3	R^6	5^3	N	R^3	5^9	Q	R^5
2^2	D^2	R^5	5^4	G	R^2	5^{10}	L	R^4
3	D^1	R^4	5^4	N	R^6	5^{10}	P	R^5
3	D^4	R^6	5^4	O^1	R^2	5^{11}	R	R^5
4^1	G	R^2	5^5	M	R^3	5^{12}	L	R^6
4^2	R	R^5	5^6	M	R^5	6	K	R^5
5^1	H^1	R^5	5^7	H^1	R^4	7	K	R^6
5^2	H^1	R^5	5^7	O^2	R^5	8	O^1	R^6
5^2	I	R^3	5^8	F	R^5			
5^2	O^2	R^5	5^8	H^2	R^5			

1787

Obv.	Rev.	Rarity	Corresponding Numbers in Hall	Obv.	Rev.	Rarity	Corresponding Numbers in Hall	Obv.	Rev.	Rarity	Corresponding Numbers in Hall
1^1	A	R^3	1^1-A	8	N	R^3	8-N	15	F	R^3	15-F*
1^1	VV	R^6	$(1^1$-VV$)$	8	O	R^3	8-O	15	R	R^6	15-R
1^2	C	R^3	1^2-C	9	D	R^4	9-D	15	S	R^5	15-S
1^3	L	R^4	1^3-L	9	E	R^4	9-E	16^1	m	R^3	16^1-M^1
1^4	WW	R^6	$(1^4$-WW$)$	9	R	R^5	9-R	16^2	NN^1	R^4	16^2-NN
2	B	R^3	2-B	10	E	R^5	10-E	16^3	l^2	R^4	16^3-L^1-2
3	G	R^5	3-G	11^1	E	R^3	11^1-E	16^4	n	R^4	16^4-N^1
4	L	C	4-L	11^2	K	R^3	11^2-K	16^5	n	R^3	16^5-N^1
5	P	R^6	5-P	11^3	K	R^6	——	16^5	p	R^5	——
6^1	M	R^1	6^1-M	12	Q	R^4	12-Q	16^5	u	R^6	——
6^2	M	R^3	6^2-M	13	D	R^3	13-D	16^6	NN^2	R^6	——
7	I	R^4	7-I	14	H	R^3	14-H	17	g^3	R^3	17-G^1-3

1787

Obv.	Rev.	Rarity	Corresponding Numbers in Hall	Obv.	Rev.	Rarity	Corresponding Numbers in Hall	Obv.	Rev.	Rarity	Corresponding Numbers in Hall
18	g^1	R^3	18-G^1-1	33^7	r^2	C	33^7-R^1-2	33^{29}	Z^7	R^4	33^{38}-Z-7
19	g^4	R^2	19-G^1-4	33^7	r^4	R^6	33^7-R^1-4	33^{29}	gg^1	R^4	33^{38}-G^2-1
20	a^2	R^3	20-A^1-2	33^7	Z^{10}	R^6	33^7-Z-10	33^{30}	EE	R^5	33^{39}-EE
21	DD	R^4	54-DD	33^8	Z^{13}	R^4	33^8-Z-13	33^{30}	SS	R^6	33^{39}-SS
22	g^2	R^5	22-G^1-2	33^8	Z^{19}	R^5	33^8-Z-19	33^{31}	gg^2	R^5	33^{37}-G^2-2
24	g^3	R^4	24-G^1-3	33^9	s^2	R^2	33^1-S^1-2	33^{32}	Z^{13}	R^1	33^{35}-Z-13
24	g^5	R^4	24-G^1-5	33^{10}	Z^7	R^5	33^4-Z-7	33^{33}	Z^3	R^4	33^{30}-Z-3
24	FF	R^6	24-FF	33^{10}	Z^8	R^4	33^4-Z-8	33^{33}	Z^{11}	R^3	33^{30}-Z-11
25	b	R^3	25-B^1	33^{10}	W^6	R^6	——	33^{34}	W^2	R^5	33^{31}-W-2
25	m	R^5	25-M^1	33^{11}	Z^{18}	R^5	33^{15}-Z-18	33^{34}	Z^3	R^5	33^{31}-Z-3
26	a^1	R^5	26-A^1-1	33^{11}	gg^1	R^5	33^{15}-G^2-1	33^{34}	Z^{11}	R^5	33^{31}-Z-11
26	kk^1	R^4	26-K^2-1	33^{12}	W^3	R^5	33^{14}-W-3	33^{35}	Z^9	R^6	33^{41}-Z-9
26	AA	R^3	26-AA	33^{12}	Z^{16}	R^8	33^{14}-Z-16	33^{36}	T^1	R^3	33^{33}-T-1
27	a^1	R^5	27-A^1-1	33^{12}	Z^{21}	R^5	33^{14}-Z-21	33^{36}	T^2	R^1	33^{33}-T-2
28	m	R^3	28-M^1	33^{12}	Z^{24}	R^6	33^{14}-Z-24	33^{36}	SS	R^6	33^{33}-SS
28	n	R^5	28-N^1	33^{13}	Z^1	R^5	33^{11}-Z-1	33^{37}	Z^9	R^3	33^{32}-Z-9
28	o	R^6	——	33^{13}	Z^6	R^4	33^{11}-Z-6	33^{38}	Z^1	R^3	33^{36}-Z-1
29^1	a^2	R^5	29-A^1-2	33^{13}	Z^7	R^4	33^{11}-Z-7	33^{38}	Z^6	R^4	33^{38}-Z-6
29^1	n	R^6	29-N^1	33^{13}	q	R^5	33^{11}-Q^1	33^{38}	Z^{18}	R^6	——
29^1	p	R^4	29-P^1	33^{13}	ff^1	R^6	33^{11}-F^2-1	33^{38}	Z^{23}	R^5	33^{38}-Z-23
29^2	N	R^6	——	33^{13}	hh^2	R^6	33^{11}-H^2-2	33^{38}	gg^1	R^5	33^{38}-G^2-1
29^2	o	R^5	51-O^1	33^{14}	Z^{14}	R^3	33^{17}-Z-14	33^{39}	Z^{20}	R^6	33^{34}-Z-20
30	hh^1	R^2	30-H^2-1	33^{15}	r^1	$\dot{R}^1$	33^5-R^1-1	33^{39}	s^1	C	33^{34}-S^1-1
30	X^1	R^3	30-X-1	33^{16}	l^2	R^4	33^6-L^1-2	33^{40}	Z^1	R^5	33^{29}-Z-1
31^1	gg^1	R^3	31^1-G^2-1	33^{16}	T^2	R^6	——	33^{40}	Z^2	R^5	33^{29}-Z-2
31^1	r^4	R^1	31^1-R^1-4	33^{16}	Z^{15}	R^1	33^6-Z-15	33^{41}	Z^{11}	R^6	33^{40}-Z-11
31^2	r^3	C	31^2-R^1-3	33^{17}	r^1	R^3	33^{13}-R^1-1	33^{42}	Z^2	R^6	33^{50}-Z-2
32^1	X^3	R^2	32^1-X-3	33^{17}	r^5	R^6	(33^{13}-R^1-5)	33^{43}	q	R^4	33^{44}-Q^1
32^2	X^1	C	32^2-X-1	33^{17}	gg^2	R^2	33^{13}-G^2-2	33^{43}	hh^2	R^4	33^{44}-H^2-2
32^2	X^2	R^1	32^2-X-2	33^{18}	Z^{24}	R^6	——	33^{44}	W^3	R^5	33^{45}-W-3
32^2	X^4	R^5	32^2-X-4	33^{19}	Z^1	C	33^{19}-Z-1	33^{45}	W^2	R^5	33^{46}-W-2
32^3	X^4	C	32^3-X-4	33^{19}	Z^2	R^3	33^{19}-Z-2	34	k^3	R^6	34-K^1-3
32^4	X^5	R^4	32^4-X-5	33^{19}	q	R^5	33^{19}-Q^1	34	ff^1	R^3	34-F^2-1
32^4	Z^3	R^5	32^4-Z-3	33^{20}	Z^9	R^4	33^2-Z-9	36	k^3	R^5	36-K^1-3
32^5	aa	R^3	32^5-A^2	33^{20}	Z^{11}	R^6	——	36	l^1	R^3	36-L^1-1
32^6	X^6	R^5	32^6-X-6	33^{21}	Z^{13}	R^6	(33^{20}-Z-13)	36	ff^2	R^5	36-F^2-2
32^7	X^1	R^5	32^7-X-1	33^{22}	II	R^6	——	37^1	cc^1	R^2	37^4-C^2-1
32^8	aa	R^5	32?-A^2	33^{23}	Z^4	R^2	33^{21}-Z-4	37^2	k^5	R^3	37^{12}-K^1-5
33^1	Z^{13}	R^4	33^{16}-Z-13	33^{23}	hh^2	R^5	33^{21}-H^2-2	37^3	i	R^2	37^9-I^1
33^1	Z^{19}	R^5	33^{16}-Z-19	33^{24}	Z^{10}	R^6	33^{22}-Z-10	37^4	k^1	R^1	37^8-K^1-1
33^2	Z^5	C	33^{12}-Z-5	33^{25}	Z^{10}	R^4	33^{25}-Z-10	37^4	RR	R^6	——
33^2	Z^{12}	C	33^{12}-Z-12	33^{25}	Z^{24}	R^5	33^{25}-Z-24	37^5	e	R^2	37^7-E^1
33^2	Z^{17}	R^4	33^{12}-Z-17	33^{25}	W^3	R^5	33^{25}-W-3	37^6	k^4	R^4	37^{11}-12^1-4
33^2	Z^{21}	R^5	33^{12}-Z-21	33^{26}	W^3	R^5	33^{26}-W-3	37^6	B	R^6	37^{11}-B
33^2	Z^{22}	R^4	33^{12}-Z-22	33^{26}	W^5	R^6	33^{26}-W-5	37^7	h^2	R^5	37^{13}-H^1-2
33^3	W^1	R^3	33^3-W-1	33^{27}	r^4	R^4	33^{23}-R^1-4	37^8	k^2	R^2	37^5-K^1-2
33^4	q	R^4	33^{18}-Q-1	33^{27}	Z^{16}	R^6	33^{23}-Z-16	37^8	HH	R^3	37^5-HH
33^4	Z^2	R^5	33^{18}-Z-2	33^{28}	Z^{11}	R^3	33^{24}-Z-11	37^8	LL	R^3	37^5-LL
33^5	T^2	R^3	33^9-T-2	33^{28}	Z^{16}	R^3	33^{24}-Z-16	37^9	e	R^3	37^6-E^1
33^6	KK	R^1	33^{10}-KK	33^{28}	Z^{20}	R^6	33^{24}-Z-20	37^{10}	RR	R^4	37^{10}-RR

1787

Obv.	Rev.	Rarity	Corresponding Numbers in Hall	Obv.	Rev.	Rarity	Corresponding Numbers in Hall	Obv.	Rev.	Rarity	Corresponding Numbers in Hall
37^{11}	ff^2	R^3	37^2-F^2-2	40	N	R^5	40-N	46	BB	R^4	46-BB
37^{12}	LL	R^4	37^1-LL	40	kk^1	R^5	40-K^2-1	47	a^3	$R^{5`}$	47-?
37^{12}	TT	R^5	37^1-TT	41	ii	R^3	41-I^2	48	g^5	R^5	48-G^1-5
37^{13}	HH	R^2	37^3-HH	42	o	R^6	42-O^1	49	Z^1	R^6	49-Z-^{1}
37^{14}	cc^2	R^6	37^{14}-C^2-2	42	kk^2	R^2	42-K^2-2	50	F	R^5	50-F*
38	GG	R^2	38-GG	43	Y	C	43-Y	(29^2	o)		51-O^1
38	l^2	R^3	38 L^1-2	44	W^4	R^2	44-W-4	52	G	R^6	52-G
39^1	h^1	R^5	39^1-H^1-1	44	W^5	R^5	44-W-5	53	FF	R^4	53-FF
39^1	ff^2	R^5	39^1-F^2-2	44	Z^{10}	R^5	44-Z-10	(21	DD)		54-DD
39^2	ee	R^4	39^2-E^2	45	CC	R^4	45-CC	55	F	R^6	(55-F*)

1788

Obv.	Rev.	Rarity	Obv.	Rev.	Rarity	Obv.	Rev.	Rarity
1	I	R^6	8	K	R^5	15^2	P	R^4
2	D	R^2	9	E	R^4	15^3	P	R^6
3^1	B^1	R^5	10	C	R^5	16^1	D	R^2
3^2	B^2	R^5	11	G	R^2	16^1	H	R^2
4^1	B^1	R^5	12^1	E	R^3	16^2	O	R^4
4^1	K	R^4	12^1	F	R^3	16^3	N	R^2
4^2	R	R^6	12^2	C	R^3	16^4	L^2	R^4
5	B^2	R^5	12^2	E	R^3	16-5	H	R^4
6	H	R^6	13	A^1	R^4	16-6	H	R^5
7	E	R^4	14^1	L^2	R^4	17	O	R^5
7	F	R^6	14^2	A^2	R^4	17	Q	R^5
7	K	R^5	15^1	L^1	R^4			

NOTE

It seems fitting that the foregoing should not be published without an expression of the loss which numismatists feel at the untimely death of the author, Mr. Henry Clay Miller, on February 6th, 1920. The preparation of the material was a great pleasure to Mr. Miller. The completed work shows the painstaking and systematic manner in which the task was done. The final manuscript revision was finished but a short time before Mr. Miller's sudden death. Some slight errors have possibly occurred in the printed pages through not having had the benefit of the Author's proof reading.

ADDITIONS AND CORRECTIONS

TO

THE STATE COINAGE OF CONNECTICUT

Published in The American Journal of Numismatics, Volume LIII, 1920

Since the publication of The State Coinage of Connecticut, several new varieties of Connecticut cents have been discovered. It has been deemed fitting to publish these, and advantage has also been taken at this time to make a number of corrections in the original article.

The Editors are indebted for most of these additions and changes to Mr. Frederick A. Canfield, of Dover, N. J., and to Mr. Hillyer Ryder, of Carmel, N. Y., for perfecting this last work of the late Henry C. Miller.

PAGE

4. 1785 cents. Type 7. No. of dies, change 1 to 2.

4. Add a reverse S to Type 5 of 1786 cents. Make 14 dies instead of 12.

5. 1785 cents. Type K. No. of dies should be 1. With obverse, omit figure 3.

5. 1786. Type D. No. dies, change 4 to 5.

5. 1786. Reverse. Make the following addition:
   Type S INDE: ET - LIB: No. of dies, 1. With obverse, 5.

6. Type 29. With Reverse column should read a^2 instead of aa.

6. Type 32. No. of dies column should read 9 instead of 8.

6. Type 37. No. of dies column should read 15 instead of 14.

6. Type 38. With Reverse column should read GG instead of gg.

6. Type 43. No. of dies column should read 2 instead of 1. With Reverse column should read X, Y.

7. Type X. No. of dies column should read 7 instead of 6. With Obverse column should read 30, 32, 43.

8. Type 12. With Reverse column add F.

9. 1787—Reverse. BB. Description should read ETLIB: (colon, not period).

9. 1788—Reverse. F should read under No. of dies column 2 instead of 1.

9. Type H. A ❋ should be placed before INDE.

9. Type R should be changed to read
   R ❋ INDE ❋ ❋ ET ❋ LIB ❋ 1 4

10. Obverse 3. Var. 1 (R^4) should be added to 3^1—L.

PAGE

11. Obverse 5. Var. 2 is now considered from the same die as Var. 1 but without the die breaks.

11. Obverse 7. Insert Var. 1 to printed description.

11. Var. 2. Similar to Var. 1; heavy break from neck through fillet ends; semicircular termination of breastplate. This is the same die as used in 4^2 of 1786. 7^2—D (R^6)

12. Reverse A. Var. 1. 6—A^1 should read 6^1—A^1.

12. Reverse D. "Four on right" should read "five on right".

13. Reverse K. Var. 1 "Bottom of I double-cut" should read "Bottom of T double-cut".

13. Var. 2 of Reverse K is now conceded to be the same as Reverse B.

14. Obverse 3. Last line, 3—D^5 (R^6) should be inserted.

14. Obverse 4. Add the words "Var. 2" after Obv. 7 in last sentence, as two varieties are now known of this 1785 cent.

15. Var. 2. Line 2. 5^2—L (R^6) should be inserted.

15. Var. 12 should be omitted as it is now considered the same as Var. 2.

15. The following new varieties are to be added:

Var. 13. Both colons incline to the right. Semicircular breastplate. Roman nose. Colons heavy and even. Upper dot of first colon low, and much larger than lower dot. Two dots between forelock and wreath. Serifs of E closed. Milling fine and ragged. 5^{13}—I (R^6)

15. Var. 14. Lower dot of first colon a little below the bottom of I. Bottom dot of second colon even with bottom of C. Colons nearly parallel with letters. Second and third N double-cut. No semicircular breastplate. Three side curls enclose dots. The curved band on armor, under fluting, on throat, tapers into almost a crescent at the ends. Milling fine. 5^{14}—S (R^6)

15. Var. 15. First colon leans to left. Upper dot very low. Lower dot even. Second colon leans to left; lower dot even; upper dot low. Letters in legend wide. A large semicircular break from rim to halfway to top of left shoulder. Surface is slightly swollen. 5^{15}—S (R^6)

17. 1786 Reverse D. Var. 5. This variety is represented by a brass casting which shows that it was recut on the letters IND, and on the milling that touches the tops of all the letters INDE. This piece shows the full device and is so small that it will lie within the milling of D^1. No original copy of this variety is known.   3—D^5 (R^6)

18. Reverse I. Last line. Add 5^{13}—I.

19. Reverse Q. Instead of "Three longitudinal lines on globe", read "There are eight longitudinal lines and three parallels of latitude on globe".

PAGE

19. Add Reverse S. INDE: ET-LIB:
Branch is thick with five small short leaves on each side of stem. End leaf about level with the middle of the base of E. Date line double. Fig. 8 touches date line; other figures are near it. Both colons are even and parallel, with upper dots low; about half as high as the adjacent letters, which are very large. Lower dot of last colon half on shield. B touches shield. Branch hand opposite D and space between N and D. The most striking feature of this reverse is a sword hilt and guard under the left elbow of the goddess. They appear to be too well formed, proportioned and located to be due to an accidental break in the die. Combined with 5^{14} and 5^{15}.

23. 1787. Obverse 26. 26—kk^2 should read 26—kk^1.

23. Obverse 27. "Last star high" should read "Last cross high".

24. Obverse 29. Var. 2. "c and o touch head" should read "c and o close to head".

25. Obverse 32. Add Var. 9. First cinquefoil close to point of bust. Second cinquefoil high and distant from period and hair. Third cinquefoil high and nearer c than wreath. Fourth cinquefoil high and near point of toga. Periods even with bottoms of adjoining letters. AUCT close, OR wide, CONNEC wide, with large c's. Second c barely touches hair; second o far from hair. Centers of last cinquefoil and period are in a straight line with lower corner of upper fillet end. 32^9—X^7

26. Var. 4. Line 4. "The lower dot nearer c." should read "The lower dot nearer I".

28. Obverse 33. Var. 16. Not the same die as Var. 14 — the second cinquefoil is lower; the third cinquefoil is more distant from c; two loops of third cinquefoil near hair; lower dot of first colon is one half below I; second cinquefoil is nearer I than is the case on 33^{14}.

30. Var. 29. "First cinquefoil entirely under bust" should read "First cinquefoil to left of bust".

31. Var. 37. Last line. Add 33^{37}—Z^{11} (R^6).

32. Var. 38. Last line. Add 33^{38}—Z^{18} (R^6).

35. Var. 14. First line. Add the word "second" before "slightly distant".

35. Add Var. 15. First fleuron small and close to left of bust. Second fleuron near hair. Third fleuron close to head, near to c, and distant from wreath. Fourth fleuron opposite space between dots of last colon — near colon and toga. First colon leans to the right — lower dot near I. Second colon parallel with c. R high. Letters widely and evenly spaced. All the c's are almost closed. 37^{15}—h^3 (R^6)

PAGE

36. Obverse 43.   Add Var. 1 to description, and add Var. 2, as follows: This is a "CONNFC" and was struck from the die before the F was changed to E and became 32^3.   The burr that was raised by the F and C punches is plainly visible. on the coin; it was removed before the altered die was used.

43^2—X^4 (R^6)

37. Obverse 50.   First line.   Change word "colon" to "period".

37. Obverse 52.   Inscription should read: AUCTORI   CONNEC.   Its rarity is 6.

40. Reverse W.   Var. 1.   The combination should read 33^3—W^1.

40. Var. 4.   Last line.   Change word "cinquefoil" to "shield".

41. Reverse X.   Var. 1.   Second line "colon" should read "period" in each case.

41. Var. 4.   Last line.   "Colon" should read "period."   Combination should read 32^2—X^4. 32^3—X^4. 43^2—X^4.

41. Var. 5.   Last line.   Change "colon" to read "period".

41. Var. 7.   First cinquefoil is distant a little more than its own width from skirt of goddess.   The next to the last cinquefoil is high and is half as far from pole as from hair.   The last cinquefoil is far from B and near shield. Last period is very weak and close to shield.   ETL are close, LIB are wide. Uprights of E and T lean to left.   Tops of both letters are long.   The upper "hole" of B is double the size of the lower "hole".   The date-line is double and unbroken.   Both 7's are low.   Top of 8 laps on lower line.   A long lock of hair floats downward and to the right from the back of the neck. The upper ribbon does not reach the pole; its triangular right hand end re- sembles the head of a snake.   The lower ribbon is in high relief and crosses in front or outside of the pole.   It looks somewhat like a horizontal break in the die.

32^9—X^7 (R^6)

42. Var. 4.   Next to last line.   Word "connected" should read "corrected".

42. Var. 6.   Fourth line.   Word "printing" should read "pointing".

43. Var. 11.   Add to combination, 33^{37}—Z^{11}.

44. Var. 13.   Add to combination, 33^{21}—Z^{13}.

45. Var. 18.   Add to combination, 33^{38}—Z^{18}.

45. Var. 20.   Combinations should read 33^{28}—Z^{20}. 33^{39}—Z^{20}.

45. Var. 21.   The second combination should read 33^{12}—Z^{21} instead of 38^{12}—Z^{21}.

47. Reverse g.   Var. 5.   "upper left" should read "upper leaf".

47. Reverse h.   Add Var. 3 — Ornament low, and on same curve as bottom of letters INDE.   Second cross midway between pole and plume.   N a little nearer to D than to I; I leans to left.   Colons parallel with adjacent letters. Upper dot of second colon low; the other dots are normal.   Lower date- line cuts top of figure 8.

37^{15}—h^3

48. Reverse k. Var. 3. First combination should read 34—k³ instead of 34—K³.

51. Reverse gg. Var. 1. Read 33²⁹—gg¹ instead of 33²⁰—gg¹.

52. Reverse BB. A colon should follow ETLIB: instead of a period. Second line should read "Lower dot of colon on shield" instead of "Period close to shield".

53. Reverse RR. 37⁷—RR should read 37⁴—RR.

54. Obverse 4. Add new combination, 4¹—B².

55. Obverse 7. 7—F should read 7—F².

55. Obverse 12. 12¹—F should read 12¹—F¹.

57. Obverse 16. Var. 4. Second line. "Colon" should read "period". Third line. "c touches head" should read "c does not touch head".

57. Var. 6. Last line. "Colon" should read "period".

57. Reverse B. Var. 2. Add combination, 4¹—B².

58. Reverse C. Third line. "Cinquefoil" should read "star".

58. Reverses E and H. On some copies the last line of these two reverses were transposed. Correct reading for Reverse E — "Narrow with small leaves." Coarse milling.   7—E. 9—E. 12¹—E. 12²—E

58. Reverse F. Place "Var. 1" before description, and make combination read 12¹—F¹.

58. Var. 2 to be added — Branch is a wheat ear — defective. Second star low and nearer to head than to T. First E double-cut. Curve of D is heavy. Top of ı is long. Ends of date-line are near milling; milling blunt. Tops of figs. 1 and 7 are below date-line and near milling. Figs. 88 lean to right and are near milling. Head and hair very crude. Break from top of head through wrist to bottom of B.   7—F² (R⁶)

58. Reverse H. Last line should read — Curve of shield and from last cinquefoil to milling.   6—H. 16¹—H. 16⁵—H. 16⁶—H

59. Reverse R. A complete description can now be given — Branch is a wheat ear and ends between D and E. Branch-hand is near lower right corner of N. Letters small and wide apart. N leans away from ı. D and E high. T leans away from E. B low and near bottom of shield. Top line of D not parallel with bottom line. First star is very low and about midway from ı to foot of goddess. Second star high and nearer forelock than to E. Third star very high and indistinct. Fourth star midway between T and L. Last star very near date-line and lower curve of shield. Fig. 1 is small — very low and distant from fig. 7, which is large. Last 8 touches date-line, which is single. All the figures lean to the right. Breaks in rim under the date. Milling crude and irregular. The legend by Hall is correct:

     * INDE *   * ET *   LIB *

Plate I

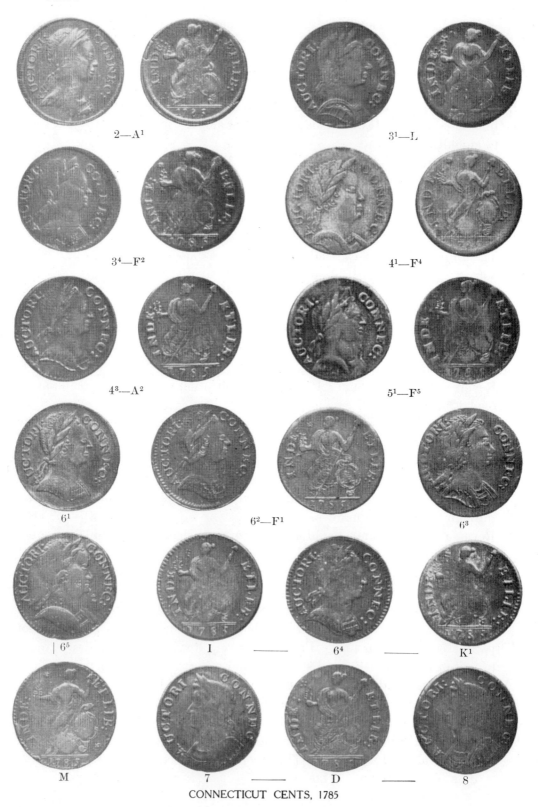

2—A¹   3¹—L

3⁴—F²   4¹—F⁴

4³—A²   5¹—F⁵

6¹   6²—F¹   6³

| 6⁵   I   ——   6⁴   ——   K¹

M   7   ——   D   ——   8

CONNECTICUT CENTS, 1785

Plate II

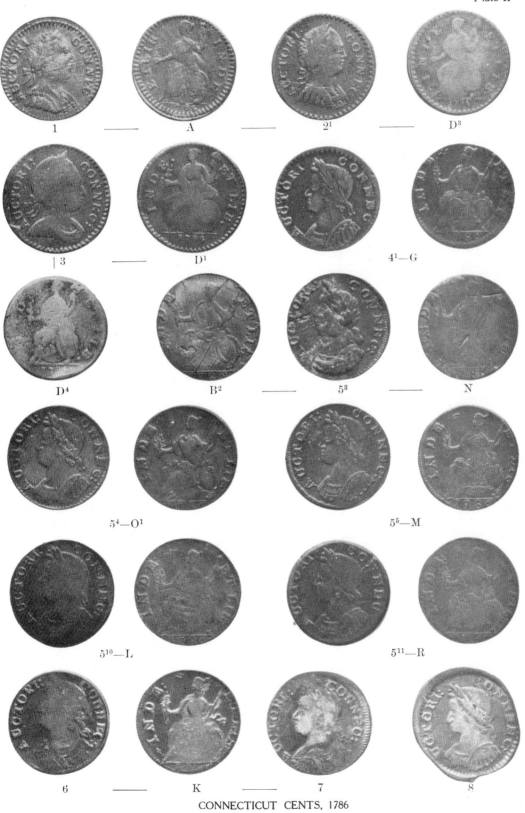

1 — A — 2¹ — D³

| 3 — D¹ — 4¹—G

D⁴ — B² — 5³ — N

5⁴—O¹ — 5⁵—M

5¹⁰—L — 5¹¹—R

6 — K — 7 — 8

CONNECTICUT CENTS, 1786

Plate III

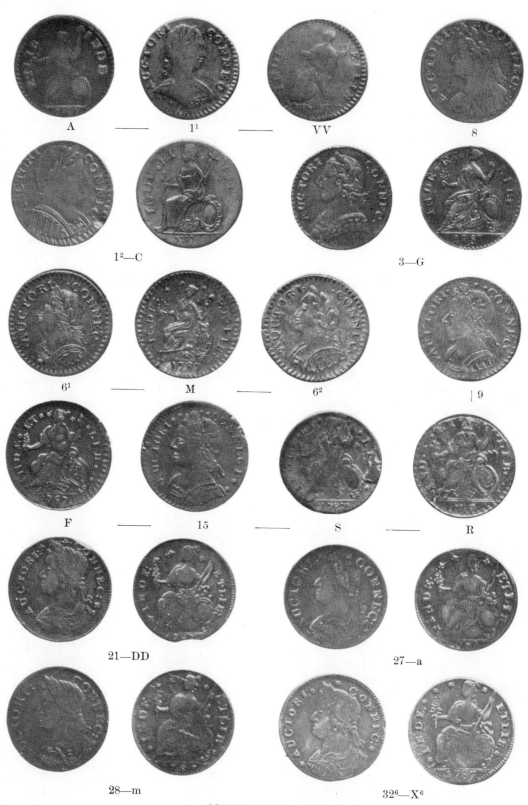

A ——— 1¹ ——— VV 8

1²—C 3—G

6¹ ——— M ——— 6² | 9

F ——— 15 ——— S ——— R

21—DD 27—a

28—m 32⁶—X⁶

CONNECTICUT CENTS, 1787

Plate IV

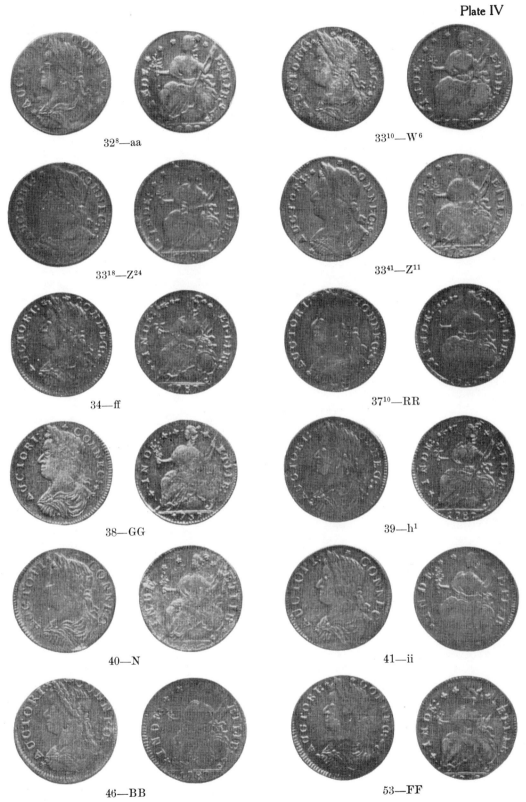

32⁸—aa   33¹⁰—W⁶

33¹⁸—Z²⁴   33⁴¹—Z¹¹

34—ff   37¹⁰—RR

38—GG   39—h¹

40—N   41—ii

46—BB   53—FF

CONNECTICUT CENTS, 1787

Plate V

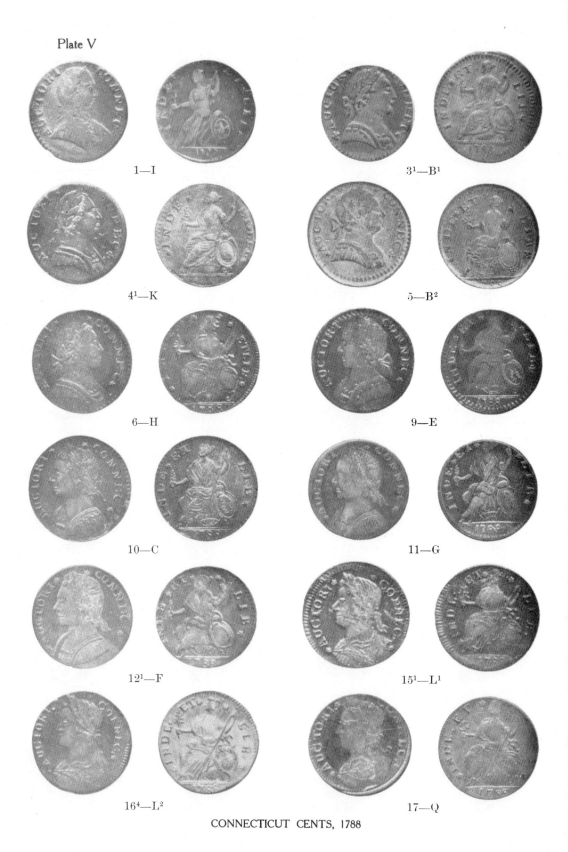

1—I

3¹—B¹

4¹—K

5—B²

6—H

9—E

10—C

11—G

12¹—F

15¹—L¹

16⁴—L²

17—Q

CONNECTICUT CENTS, 1788

EXTRAORDINARY VARIETY COLLECTION
OF CONNECTICUT COPPERS

It is with the utmost pride that we present this collection of Connecticut coppers, one of the finest ever put together for condition and simultaneously exceptionally complete—containing over 92% of the known varieties. **At present the only collections which could conceivably give this one any competition for completeness are the Canfield bequest in the museum of the American Numismatic Society, and the Barnsley collection; however, the present collection contains varieties not represented in either of these.** It was built up over more than 15 years, varieties being added from several of the major auctions in addition to large groups from the Norman Bryant and Theodore L. Craige estates and the famous Stephen Hoard. As a result, **many specimens herein included are believed to be finest known of their variety, and literally dozens will qualify in the condition census** (defined as the six finest of each variety).

This claim is far more important than it sounds. It is common now to hear collectors of early or late large cents speak of their coins as condition census or even finest knowns. Those series have been explored in detail, and they are popular enough that literally hundreds of auctions have contained important groups. However, in colonial coppers the picture is completely different, especially among Connecticuts. Reference books in the series have been confined to reprintings of the unsatisfactory and difficult Miller text (1920), many varieties have never before been illustrated (a feature remedied in the present catalogue), many rarities have thus remained unrecognized, and worst of all the vast majority of Connecticut coppers were weakly struck on defective planchets so that only parts of the designs show. **The usual grade range for the entire 1785–88 series is Poor to About Fine, the average single grade being Good to VG,** even among the 27 varieties which can be classed as common (i.e. more than 500 survivors estimated).

A strictly Fine Connecticut copper is unusual; a VF is automatically scarce, an EF or better is by definition a rarity and far more important than suspected, and any Connecticut with even a remote claim to mint state is a great rarity with four figure potential, despite the Stepney Hoard (many of whose coins were not full unc.). Auctions which contained choice Connecticuts during the last sixty years can be counted on the fingers of one hand; Miller (1920), New Netherlands 51st (1958), New Netherlands 60th (1968), Merkin (Oct. 31, 1973). In addition, smaller important groups were included in the Stack's Oct. 1970, Feb. and March 1973 auctions (second from the Norman Bryant estate, first and third from the Appleton—Mass. Historical Society collection). Other auctions have routinely contained only a few, mostly as type coins and in lower grades. The Dr. Hall, Wurtzbach, Ryder, Boyd, Virgil Brand, Craige, Bryant, and Bowers collections were all privately dispersed over the years, as the Stepney Hoard, and no records were released of the prices realized; for which reason few records exist even for the commoner varieties, and none at all for some of the rarities.

VIEWED IN THIS LIGHT, THE BARE STATISTICS OF THIS FANTASTIC COLLECTION BECOME AWESOME.

1785. Of 27 varieties with mailed bust right, this colection contains 25, most ranking in the condition census. Of **4** varieties reported to exist with mailed bust left, **3** are represented and we have no description of the fourth; all rank among the finest.

1786. Of 8 reported varieties with mailed bust right, this collection contains 6, all of Condition Census level and all rare but one. **Of 30 varieties with mailed bust left, this collection contains 28, almost all in the condition census. Both Draped Bust varieties are represented,** both being very rare and among the finest known; so far as we know, this is the first time since the Miller sale that both have shown up simultaneously in auction.

1787. Of 9 mailed bust right varieties known, this collection contains 7, all qualifying in the condition census. Of the 23 with mailed bust left, 22 are here and almost all are in the census. Of the 23 different draped bust varieties confirmed to exist, this collection contains 187, the largest offering in auction history; almost all are condition census level.

1788. All 9 mailed bust right varieties are represented, including the exceedingly rare 1–L with the Vermont reverse, mostly in the condition census, **as are all 12 known mailed bust left varieties.** All but one of the 15 draped bust left varieties are here, mostly again in the census. In all, 315 out of 342 varieties, representing all six of the mints known to have struck Connecticut coppers. The mint of issue is specified for the groups of varieties below, for the first time in auction history.

Unless otherwise mentioned, all specimens here offered have complete legends and dates. They normally come with a variety of planchet lamination defects or planchet cracks, these being inherent to the manufacturing of these coins. They normally come with local weaknesses, though in the present collection many specimens will be free of them. Some show Miller attributions marked in red or white ink, either on edge or field or occasionally on the face. This was a practice of the oldest collectors wishing to avoid the difficult task of reattributing these coins once the die variety had been correctly identified for once and all; it does not constitute damage but should rather be taken as evidence that the coins are from old specialist holdings, most often either Dr. Thomas Hall or Henry Clay Miller.

All specimens have been photographed and are illustrated here, many for the first time in numismatic history. However, no photograph could do justice to the lustrous surfaces of many coins here graded even Extremely Fine; weak striking is often found on coins showing mint surface or even traces of original mint red. **Only personal examination of a large number of these coins will enable you to familiarize yourself with the way Connecticut coppers normally come and to appreciate the extraordinary quality of the present offering.**

For your information we provide you with this chart as a guideline:

RARITY CHART
Approximate number known

R1 — More than 1,250	R5 — 31 to 75
R2 — 501 to 1,250	R6 — 13 to 20
R3 — 201 to 500	R7 — 4 to 12
R4 — 76 to 200	R8 — 2 or 3

Unique 1

RAHWAY, N. J. MINT

This was the legal mint established for coining "Horse Head" coppers for the State of New Jersey, from November 1786 through June 1788. It was a grist mill and sawmill owned by Assemblyman Daniel Marsh, on King's Highway at the Rahway River, then part of Elizabethtown; the exact location is at St. George's Ave. and School Street, Rahway, recently occupied by Koos Bros. Department Store, and the site is marked by a plaque erected on April 20, 1954, reading First Mint Site; a new marker reads Rahway Mint. The legal coiners, Alboin Cox (later Assayer of the U. S. Mint) and Thomas Goadsby, under their sponsor and bondsman Matthias Ogden, began coinage late in November 1786, using first Benjamin Dudley and later James F. Atlee as diecutters. They had to pay 10% of their output directly into the state treasury, or the equivalent in "lawful money" which effectively meant New Jersey paper money. Finding themselves in financial trouble from the start, they resorted the dodge of making Connecticut coppers, imitating the 1785 bust right type then common, and sending people to buy supplies in Connecticut and New York with quantities of these coins, if possible moving bags of them for Spanish or Mexican silver. The bust right coins of 1786, punched–linked with the New Jersey cents from this mint and with other early James F. Atlee dies, are correctly attributed to this mint. There was no law against the practice, and the Rahway coiners did not have to pay any tithe to either New Jersey or Connecticut on these coins. This enterprise ended about June 1, 1787 when Atlee left for Machin's Mill, and Albion Cox was arrested and put into debtor's prison on suit of his ex–partner Thomas Goadsby and Samuel Atlee, the latter one of the Machin's Mills partners, apparently for nonpayment of James Atlee for dies. Goadsby then took over the Rahway mint equipment; Matthias Ogden bailed Cox out but was unable to keep him out of debtor's prison, especially after Benjamin Dudley sued him for back wages. Ogden obtained a court order forcing Goadsby to return the mint equipment after which he, Ogden, ran the mint by himself in Elizabethtown until well into 1789; in the meantime Albion Cox had managed to get onto a boat bound for England, being persuaded with difficulty to return in 1792 as Assayer of the Mint.

We may assume that the Connecticut coins of 1786 with mailed bust right, made in Rahway, N. J., between January and May 1786, were the coins alluded to in the bill May 1786 quoted by Crosby, p. 220, as "base and Counterfeit Copper Coin . . . already imported and circulating in this State". This bill proposed to levy a fine of £10 Lawful Money per offense on anyone importing more than 50 copper coins of any kind other than genuine Connecticut coppers or any other legal state coppers or any later coins to be issued by the Confederation; it was passed by the lower house of the Connecticut Assembly, but failed to pass the state senate.

To have reached official attention of this kind, the quantity must have been considerable, probably a few tens of thousands to judge from the number of dies (4 obvs., 5 revs.). They are presumably the reason for all later **legal** Connecticuts having bust to **left.** Only one of these is readily obtainable (M. 2.1–A).

1787

The coinages of this year are by far the most complicated of all Colonial issues. To simplify the presentation, and to encourage collectors who might have been daunted by the indigestible mess of Miller descriptions, we have subdivided the issues of this year first by **mints** and thereunder by designs.

The mints striking Connecticuts dated 1787 are as follows:

Unlocated Private Mint

Responsible for the "Muttonhead" coins, M. 1.2—C, 1.2—mm, time unknown. These are stylistically unlike anything else in the Colonial series.

Morristown, New Jersey

Dies by Walter Mould, between June 1787 and August 1788. Responsible for the two "Laughing Head" varieties and those punchlinked with them; note the peculiar wide horse-shoe-shaped U, which is among the letters shared by these coins and the wide-planchet New Jersey cents of 1787–88. Mould, a pupil of the Wyons in Birmingham, England, emigrated to the USA in 1786 (bringing with him a number of dies, some by Wyon including the IMMUNE COLUMBIA and several prototype dies for the New Jersey coinage). He associated himself with Albion Cox and Thomas Goadsby, and with Revolutionary War hero Matthias Ogden as surety, entered into a contract with the State of New Jersey to establish an official mint for making copper coins, commonly miscalled cents but correctly termed coppers. Mould quarreled with the others and Ogden got the legislature to pass a special act allowing him to coin his million N. J. coppers separately from the Cox–Goadsby two million. Mould moved to Morristown, leasing the John Cleve Symmes house "Solitude", and struck his full million N. J. coppers, of which he paid a tithe (a 10% commission) to the state treasurer, in coppers or paper currency rather than in silver or gold—in addition to coining tens of thousands, possibly hundreds of thousands, of Connecticut coppers, on which he paid no tax or commission whatever. These varieties are all identified and all four are here offered.

Machin's Mills near Newburgh, N. Y.
(June 1787 through early 1700)

Dies by James F. Atlee, who joined the staff of this notorious "Manufactory of Hard Ware" in the former month. Operations, under Capt. Thomas Machin and a half dozen or so other partners, were kept secret and largely went on at night; according to Eric P. Newmen, workmen wore hideous masks to frighten away local children. Much of the firm's output consisted of imitation halfpence of George III popularly known as "Tory Pennies," some of which were offered in earlier Pine Three auctions. Later, the firm negotiated a contract with the legal Vermont coinage franchise holders, splitting profits 60-40 in favor of Machin's Mills, in order that the Vermont enterprise could use the die-cutting services of Atlee—accounting for the Vermont reverse found on 1788 Connecticut cent variety 1-I. The firm also made coppers purporting to be New Jersey and Connecticut issues; we here offer 8 of the 9 known 1787 Connecticut varieties from this mint.

"The Company for Coining Coppers"
New Haven I
Through June 1, 1787

Dies by Abel Buel, possibly with assistants who may have included his son Benjamin, on behalf of Samuel Bishop, Joseph Hopkins, James Hillhouse and James Goodrich—the legal franchise holders. As Abel Buel had turned over the 1786 hubs to his other son William, who took them to Vermont, the earliest dies of 1787 from the New Haven mint were left–over 1786 obverses (Miller die 1786 5, 3, the "Hercules," becoming 1787 die 7; 1786 die 7, the second Draped Bust, becoming 1787 die 29.1) together with a few hand–cut dies (1787 obvs. 8, 9); shortly afterward, Buel completed a mailed bust hub (for obvs. 2, 5, 10–15) which he later gave to his son Benjamin (see introduction to 1788, below). After James Jarvis bought a controlling interest in the Company for Coining Coppers, **it ceased legal operations** as such, becoming that next to follow.

Jarvis & Co.
(June 1, 1787–Fall 1788)

Dies at first by Abel Buel, than by apprentices using his hubs. These coins are punch–linked with the FUGIO cents, sharing the cinquefoil and fleuron ornaments, numeral and letter punches of the latter, Jarvis had bought into the Company to have a legitimate base of operations for making some 30,666,666 FUGIO cents (345 tons at 157.5 grains per coin), for which he had by bribery obtained a federal contract, plus some 71,174½ lbs. copper which he had bought from the goverment at 11¼d. sterling per pound (but never paid for); the whole scandalous story is told by Taxay, **U. S. Mint and Coinage,** 28–38. Finding difficulties in obtaining local equipment for making copper blanks and dies on the scale contemplated, Jarvis went to England in February 1788 to try to negotiate a contract with Matthew Boulton (of Boulton & Watt's Soho Mint near Birmingham—the Watt was steam–engine inventor James Watt), but Boulton would have nothing to do with him unless Jarvis could somehow furnish security in something other than depreciated Continental notes or promissory notes. In his absence, his employees used the mint (and the federal copper) for making Connecticuts, the vast majority of 1787–88 draped bust coins being made under these auspices, including the standard 33–Z type of which some 48 obv. and 25 rev. dies are known; the texture of the copper indicates that either the same source provided metal for FUGIO and Connecticut blanks, or that the remainder of the federal copper was used to make Connecticuts too.

Despite Jarvis & Co's token delivery of some 398,577 FUGIO coppers weighing 8,968 lbs; some time shortly before May 21, 1788, the federal authorities became aware that Jarvis was in default and voided his contracts as of Sept. 16, 1788, whereupon Jarvis promptly went back to Europe. On Feb 24, 1791, Secretary of Treasury, Alexander Hamilton sued Jarvis for breach of contract, obtaining a judgement of $20,000 Spanish plus damages, but not one cent was ever collected. Some time after Sept. 1788, representatives of Machin's Mill bought the Jarvis & Co. equipment.

We have found it necessary to depart from the Crosby—Miller classification scheme, which treated misspellings, omitted colons or ornaments, etc., as intentional type changes. The procedure here is to make groups of those varieties sharing the same punches and ornaments, producing a coherent sequence which seems to be fairly close to the chronological order as the latter was determined by die break evidence. However, within the earlier groups, we have found it necessary to use the Miller order of obverses so long as Miller numbers are being used. In a subsequent book we hope to adopt a less cumbersome numbering system and to justify some of the more controversial historical and other conclusions here summarized, describing and picturing the few varieties not here offered. The numerous and popular misspellings and other die blunders, which have rendered the Connecticut series attractive to many collectors, testify to the use of apprentices not too careful about which punches they picked up, or who sometimes failed to correct a broken punch. Actually, five problems are reflected by these blunders:

1. Spacing problems—AUCTORI CONNECT, IND ET LIB.

2. Wrong choice of punch—AUCIORI, AUCTOBI, CONNFC, CONNLC, ETIIB, INDL, ETLIR (sometimes)

3. Broken punch not corrected—AUCTOPI, ETLIR (sometimes).

4. Corrected blunders—"FNDE" (INDE over FU), and overdate revs. Q,R.

5. Emergency substitutes for broken or unavailable punches— CONNEC/FC ET/FT, LIB/LIR, B made by combining R and L, etc.

Among these, the wrong choice of punch represents the most serious blunder and thus the most popular, though the other classes contain far rarer varieties. Most spacing problems were "solved" by adding or omitting ornaments and/or by crowding letters or allowing them to spread out as they came. The "FNDE" indicates that an apprentice fresh from lettering a FUGIO die allowed habit to overcome him before he realized that this die blank bore a seated figure, not a sundial. Both "overdates", Q (1787/1877) and R (1787/1788), represent blunders, not mint economy; the group including these is associated with another spacing problem—branch dividing IN DE—thought to be among Benjamin Buel's earliest work during the last days of the Company for Coining Coppers just before Jarvis takeover.

JARVIS & CO. (NEW HAVEN II)
Draped Bust Design, Small Letters

The inception date of this mint may be taken as June 1, 1787, when James Jarvis, the holder of a federal contract to coin FUGIO cents, acquired a majority (56¼%) of the stock of the reorganized "Company for Coining Coppers." At that date the Company, no longer operated by the original franchise holders, ceased legal coinage of Connecticut coppers; the owners, James Jarvis (9/16), Mark Leavenworth (⅛), Abel Buel (⅛) and John Goodrich (1/16), were organized to make FUGIO coins, dismissing the supervisory committee of Inspection (David Austin, Ebenezer Chittenden, Isaac Beers). However, they redoubled their output of Connectcuts instead, delivering one load of FUGIO cents (some 398,577 pieces) to the federal authorities. This mint's

product is identified by the distinctive smaller letters than any previously in use, the F, U, I and O punches (the F usually but not always corrected to E in the working dies) being identical on its Connecticuts and on its FUGIO obverses; the dates are identical, and both classes of coins shade the same large and small fleurons and cinquefoil ornaments. The copper is of much the same texture as well.

Reasons for this highly irregular procedure, which was to result in the federal governments suing Jarvic for some $20,000 for default, are not far to seek. Connecticut coppers were a readily accepted article in trade and would yield a living while preparations were in progress for the projected (castles–in–Spain) mintage of over 30,000,000 FUGIO coppers. Jarvis obtained some 71,174½ lbs. of copper from the government at 11 pence sterling per lb., for which he did not pay a cent; in his absence, to show good faith, representatives of his mint in May 1788 delivered some 398,577 FUGIO cents weighing 8,968 lbs. to the Treasurer of the United States. In the meantime, with Jarvis's consent, the mint people under Jarvis's father–in–law Samuel Broome and his partner Jeremiah Platt, coined the remaining 62,206½ lbs. of copper into Connecticut coins, strictly contrary to contract. If these weighed the legal 144 grains each, they would have comprised some 3,023,927 pieces; Crosby indicates that they are usually a little lightweight, so that the total issue from Jarvis & Co. may have been as high as 3½ million or more.

A first Buel may have supervised diemaking operations, but it is almost certain that he spent almost no time at the mint especially after the fraud had begun of making Connecticuts using federal copper—Buel had already been in enough trouble with the law in his earlier years, having a cropped ear and a brand mark to show for it. In view of the frequent blundered dies, probably only apprentices and ordinary laborers completed the dies from Buel's hubs. As of Sept. 16, 1788 Congress voided the defaulted FUGIO contract, leaving Jarvis & Co. with no legal status whatever save that Buel retained a ⅛ share of the original franchise to make Connecticut coppers. Realizing that the federal authorities might come after him because of the use of federal copper to make Connecticut coins on Jan 21, 1789, he deeded his house to James Jarvis and his share in the franchise to his son Benjamin, including the mailed bust left hub with triple leaves, and left for England, not to return until 1791. In the meantime, Jarvis and Samuel Broome went to Paris to try to set up a subsidiary of Boulton's mint.

At some unknown date after September 16, 1788, representatives of Machin's Mills bought the remaining equipment of Jarvis & Co., including presses, the draped bust hub and its corresponding reverse (both now in barely usable condition), several completed dies and punches—accounting for such odd combinations as 1788 M. 16.1–D, which mules a typical Jarvis obverse of latest style with one of Atlee's Machin's Mill dies earlier found with a GEORGIVS III REX obverse.

As of June 20, 1789, any and all former legal coiners' franchises were suspended indefinitely by a show–cause order passed by the Connecticut State Assembly.

The mint location is not precisely known. Crosby (p. 210) quoted one Henry Meigs (1854) as having visited a mint in New Haven while it was making Connecticut coppers **in 1788,** which date if accurate can only refer to Jarvis & Co. Earlier mints had already ceased operation, except for Machin's Mills and possibly Morristown, N. J.; Benjamin Buel had not yet begun to coin on his own. Meigs specifically mentioned Samuel Broome, which is confirmatory—Broome in supervisory capacity (in Jarvis's absence), concluding that he must have had a subcontract for coining Connecticuts (after all, a completely clandestine operation would not openly have given samples to children lest they reveal its location). We may therefore identify as the Jarvis Mint the one "at Morris Cove, . . . on the right hand side of the harbor . . . about two miles above the light house," "under the Southern Bluff, near the center of the north shore of the harbor in New Haven." If the Westville Mint, cited by Bushnell (Crosby, p. 211). was a legal mint for Connecticut coppers, it was most probably the original site of the 1785–87 Company for Coining Coppers at one or other of its various reorganizational states.

There are three major divisions of Jarvis Mint coins, each with various subdivisions:

I. Crosses on reverse, no other ornaments

    A. Crosses on obv.

    B. Fleurons on obv.

II. "Composite ornament." following INDE: (large pellet, large fleuron, small fleuron, leaf)

    A. Crosses on obv.

    B. No obv. ornaments.

    C. Large obv. fleurons.

    D. Small obv. fleurons (as on those to follow unless noted), two rev. crosses.

    E. Rev. cross and scroll.

    F. Two rev. scrolls.

    G. Paired rev. fleurons.

Transitional Group H. Obv. Cinquefoils, Rev. Composite Ornament. Transitional Group I. Small fleurons. Rev. Cinquefoils, altered from crosses. Transitional (?) Group J. Small Fleurons. Rev. Old "Company" Reverses.

II. Cinquefoils both sides, no other ornaments.

    A. Two cinquefoils after INDE: some cinquefoils either side altered from corsses.

    B. Same but obv. normal.

    C. Two normal cinquefoils after INDE: Colon stamps both sides.

    D. Three cinquefoils after INDE: Colon stops both sides.

    E. Transitional. Same but colons one side, periods the other.

    F. Same but period stops both sides.

As in previous issues, these classes of ornaments are believed to identify the different workmen who completed the dies from Buel's hubs. A very few varieties (Transitional group II J) used old worn or rusted dies of the "Company for Coining Copperfs" (M. 37.6–B, 37.8–LL, 37.12–LL), but aside from these, the groups are reasonably well circumscribed. The group with crosses came first because cross ornaments were used on earlier Company dies; those with cinquefoils are last because several of these obverses were reused in 1788, and many 1788–dated dies use the same punches. This remark applies especially to certain obverses of type 32 of 1787 which became type 16 or 1788—period stops only.

More survive of division III than of all other Connecticuts put together; more varieties of the standard 33–Z type (Group III

D with all four colons present) exist than of all other Draped Busts put together. Incredible haste and carelessness mark division III; many blanks are exceptionally defective, many dies broke almost immediately, producing great rarities; others show obvious blunders and corrected blunders—several of them earlier alluded to, others less well known such as E of INDE corrected from N, CONNEC with E corrected from F, ETLIB with B corrected from R, others with B punched over a cinquefoil.

1788

The coinages bearing this date include many rarities, some of these were not known until recently in good enough condition even for proper identification. Even now, the preservation of some survivors is not good enough for absolute assignment to mint of issue. The question of mint is further complicated by the fact that Machin's Mills representative bought out the equipment (including used and unused dies) of both Jarvis & Co. and Benjamin Buel. The mints known to have struck Connecticut coppers dated 1788 are as follows:

JARVIS & CO.
MORRIS COVE, NEW HAVEN AREA
(THROUGH ABOUT SEPTEMBER 1788)

Operations continued from 1787, in the absence of James Jarvis, under supervision of Samuel Broome, his father-in-law. Output consisted of Draped Bust coins, from the old Abel Buel hubs, though some of the coins were dated 1787. Copper sources included the remainder of the 71,174½ lbs. of federal copper discussed in the introductions to 1787 and to Jarvis & Co. under that date; but many of the 1788 coins were evidently made from copper of different source, as the texture is completely different. Different apprentices worked on these dies and presses from those of 1787. As of Sept. 16, 1788, federal authorities voided Jarvis's contract for nonfulfillment, whereupon Jarvis (who had just returned from Europe) promptly abandoned the mint and took the next boat for France. Broome and associates, having no legal entitlement to coin either Connecticut or the federal government (their Connecticut franchise having been of dubious legality) at some unknown date, probably in September 1788, sold presses, punches, hubs, and some working dies, to representatives of Machin's Mills.

MACHIN'S MILLS
NEAR NEWBURGH, N. Y.
(THROUGH EARLY 1790)

Principal output consisted of "Tory Pennies", imitation halfpence of George III, dated 1774, 1776, 1778, 1787, 1788 and a few other dates. After the 1787 agreement with the legal Vermont coiners, this mint furnished dies for the Rupert (Vermont) mint, later in 1788 also issuing Vermont coppers on its own, using dies by James F. Atlee. One of the regular 1788 Vermont reverses, Ryder 25 (also found on 28 and 29), was taken back to Newburgh and subsequently used with a GEORGIVS III REX obverse from the same head punch as the Vermonts (commonly called Vermont Ruyer 31), then with the old Connecticut small bust right die of 1787 (Miller .1.1), forming the 1788 combination 1-I, a major

rarity proudly offered here. In August 1788, Machin's Mills representatives bought the equipment which was being abandoned by
Walter Mould of the Morristown, N.J., mint, just before he managed to flee the state to avoid debtor's prison. We have also seen
that this firm later bought the remaining Jarvis & Co. equipment.
This accounts for the varieties muling Atlee's reverse D of 1788
with old Jarvis & Co. draped bust obverses, making the combinations known as 1788 Miller 16.1–D, 16.1–H, 16.5–H.

BENJAMIN BUEL
NEW HAVEN (?)
April 1787 (?)

On Jan. 21, 1789, Abel Buel deeded his house to James Jarvis
and his remaining ⅛ share in the original Connecticut "Company
for Coining Coppers" to his son Benjamin, and promptly left for
England, not to return until 1791. The reason is not known with
certainty, but the timing suggests that Abel Buel might well have
realized the precariousness of his position (see above, 1787, introduction to Jarvis & Co. issues). Young Benjamin began striking
Connecticut coppers on his own account, using the old abandoned
Triple Leaves mailed bust hub of 1787 and the reverse puncheon
with Ms. Liberty holding a wheat ear, neither one known to have
been used by Jarvis & Co.

The state assembly's show–cause order of May 1789 effectively
ended all remaining franchises, including Benjamin Buel's as of
June 20, 1789, after which no more Connecticut coppers could
legally be coined. At some later date, Benjamin Buel's equipment
was sold to representatives of Machin's Mills, accounting for the
presence of a Buel wheat–ear reverse R among the varieties correctly attributed to Machin's Mill (M. 4.2–R). Benjamin Buel's
Connecticuts must have been very limited in quantity; as many of
them are overstrikes on other coins, clearly adequate copper supplies must have been a problem for him even more than some
of the earlier mints.

PLATES AND DATA

Coins illustrated on the new plates (pages 93–124) are as they appeared in the Famous Pine Tree Auction, February 15, 1975, and are reprinted here with related data courtesy of Dr. Stanley Apfelbaum, President, First Coinvestors, Inc., and Pine Tree Auction Company, Inc. The numerals under each coin illustrated is the lot number as it appeared in the auction. Overall supervision for the catalog was by Mr. Walter Breen.

THE COINS OF 1785

Lot No.	Miller Number	Rarity	Prices Realized
1	M1-E	6	$ 150
2	M2-A-1	3	$ 130
3	M2-A.4	3	$ 73
4	M3.1-A.3	3	$ 125
5	M3.1-F.3(a)	8	$ 140
6	M3.1-L	4	$ 140
7	M3.2-L	3	$ 300
8	M3.3-F.3	4	$ 110
9	M3.4-F.1	3	$ 75
10	M3.4-F.2	3	$ 260
11	M3.5-B	2	$ 66
12	M4.1-F.4	1	$ 700
13	M4.3-A.2	3	$ 75
14	M4.3-D	4	$ 45
15	M4.4-C	5	$ 450
16	M4.4-D	6	$ 220
17	M5-F.5	5	$ 550
18	M6-1-A.1	4	$ 75
19	M6.2-F.1	4	$ 300
20	M6.3-G.1	3	$ 125
21	M6.3-G.2	4	$ 325
22	M6.4-F.5	6	$130
23	M6.4-I	4	$ 140
24	M6.4-K	6	$ 185
25	M6.5-M	5	$ 160
26	M7.1-D	6	$ 210
27	M7.2-D	7	$ 815
29	M8-D	7	$ 750

THE COINS OF 1786

30	M1-A	6	$ 725
31	M2.-1-A	3	$ 260
32	M2.1-D.3	8	$ 285
33	M2.2-D.2	7	$ 450
35	M3.-D.1	6	$ 225
36	M.3-D.4	8	$ 135
37	M4.1-G	2	$ 130
38	M4.2-R	7	$ 170
39	M4.2-S	8(b)	$ 225
40	M5.1-H.1	6	$ 415
41	M5.2-H.1	6	$ 145
42	M5.2-I	3	$ 110
43	M5.2-L	7(c)	$ 445
44	M5.2-0.2	6	$ 320
45	M5.4-G	2	$ 135
46	M5.4-N	7	$ 210
47	M5.4-0.1	2	$ 475
48	M5.5-M	3	$ 100
49	M5.6-M	6	$ 185
50	M5.7-H.1	5	$ 160
51	M5.7-0.2	6	$ 160
52	M5.8-F	6	$ 675
53	M5.8-H.2	6	$ 160
54	M5.8-0.2	4	$ 55
55	M5.9-B.1	6	$ 110
56	M5.9-0	6	$ 345
57	M5.9-L	8(d)	$ 465
58	M5.10-L	5	$ 200
59	M5.10-P	6	$ 310
60	M5.11-R	6	$ 360
61	M5.14-S	7	$ 590
62	M5.3-B.2	8	$ 620
63	M5.3-6	7	$ 240
64	M5.3-N	4	$ 550
65	M6-K	6	$ 550
66	M7-K	7	$ 290

THE COINS OF 1787

67	M1.2-C	6	$ 145
69	M1.2-C	4	$ 160
70	M1.3-L	7	$ 275

71	M4-L	1	$ 375
73	M6.1-M	1	$ 260
74	M6.2-M	1	$ 200
75	M1.1-A	3	$ 525
76	M1.1-VV	7	$ 170
77	M52-G.2	8(e)	$ 850
78	M52-G.1	7	$ 310
79	M3-G.1	7	$ 325
80	M13-D	4	$ 140
81	M32.4-F	7	$ 315
82	M50-F	7	$ 425
83	M7	6	$ 650
84	M8-N	4	$ 100
85	M8-O	4	$ 55
86	M9-D	6	$ 180
87	M9-E	5	$ 150
88	M9-R	7	$ 400
89	M11.1-E	2	$ 250
90	M11.2-K	4	$ 75
91	M11.3-K	8	$ 180
92	M2-B	3	$ 70
93	M10-E	7	$ 185
94	M14-H	4	$ 475
95	M5-P	7	$ 185
96	M12-Q	6	$ 375
97	M15-F	4	$ 160
97A	M15-F	4	$ 500
98	M15-R	7	$ 775
99	M15-S	7	$ 400
100	M16.1-M	3	$ 65
101	M16.2-NN.1	5	$ 185
102	M16.4-N	6	$ 185
103	M16.5-N	4	$ 290
104	M16.5-P	7	$ 240
105	M16.6-NN2	7	$ 235
106	M28-M	3	$ 130
107	M28-N	7	$ 275
108	M28-O	7	$ 175
109	M29.1-N	7	$ 200
110	M29.1-P	6	$ 250
111	M29.2-N	7	$ 300
112	M29.2-O	7	$ 170
113	M40-N	7	$ 375

114	M40-KK.1	6	$ 135
115	M41-ii	4	$ 210
116	M42-O	7	$ 175
117	M42-KK.2	3	$ 60
118	M25-M	6	$ 350
119	M26-KK.1	6	$ 125
120	M29.1-a.2	7	$ 375
121	M20-A.2	4	$ 270
122	M25-b	4	$ 125
123	M26-a.1	6	$ 325
123A	M26-a.1	6	
124	M26-AA	4	$ 90
125	M27-a.1	7	$ 235
126	M56-BB	5	$ 160
127	M47-a.3	7	$ 245
128	M17-g.3	4	$ 60
129	M18-g.1	4	$ 425
130	M19-g.4	3	$ 140
131	M21-DD	6	$ 135
132	M22-g.2	7	$ 250
133	M24-g.3	5	$ 135
134	M24-g.5	6	$ 160
135	M24-EF	7	$ 225
136	M38-GG	3	$ 150
137	M45-CC	6	$ 145
138	M48-g.5	7	$ 175
139	M53-FF	5	$ 275
140	M38-1.2	4	$ 70
141	M16.3-1.2	6	$ 250
142	M34-ff.1	4	$ 50
143	M34-K.3	8	$ 225
144	M37.5-e	4	$ 800
145	M37.7-h2	6	$ 170
146	M37.9-e	4	$ 600
147	M37.15-h3	8(f)	$ 225
148	M39.1-h.1	6	$ 140
149	M37.3-i	3	$ 90
150	M37.1-cc.1	4	$ 90
151	M37.2-K.5	5	$ 180
152	M37.4-K.1	2	$ 450
153	M37.6-K.4	6	$ 150
154	M37.8-K.2	3	$ 125
155	M37.14-cc.2	8	$ 300

156	M48-4.3	8(g)	$ 400
157	M36-1.1	4	$ 90
158	M36-ff.2	7	$ 260
159	M37.8-HH	4	$ 150
160	M37.10-RR	6	$ 325
161	M37.11-ff.2	4	$ 75
162	M37.13-HH	3	$ 110
163	M39.1-ff.2	6	$ 175
164	M39.2-ee	6	$ 150
165	M56-xx	8(h)	$ 325
167	M33.13-ff.1	8	$ 375
168	M33.16-1.2	6	$ 325
169	M33.21-K.4	8(i)	$ 400
170	M37.12-TT	7	$ 225
171	M37.6-B	7	$ 135
172	M37.8-LL	5	$ 60
173	M37.12-LL	5	$ 160
173A	M37.12-LL	5	$ 400
174	M33.30-EE	7	$ 175
175	M33.30-SS	8(j)	$ 210
176	M33.21-EE	8(k)	$ 325
177	M33.36-SS	8(l)	$ 350
178	M33.47-TT	8(m)	$ 475
179	M33.9-s.2	3	$ 60
180	M33.39-S.1	1	$ 200
181	M33.5-T.2	4	$ 45
182	M33.16-T.2	8	$ 200
183	M33.36-T.1	4	$ 200
184	M33.36-T.2	2	$ 275
185	M33.36-T.3	8(n)	$ 425
186	M33.11-gg.1	6	$ 300
187	M33.29-gg.1	6	$ 260
188	M33.38-gg.1	7	$ 150
189	M33.17-gg.2	3	$ 60
190	M33.31-gg.2	7	$ 195
191	M33.7-4.2	1	$ 200
192	M33.7-r	7	$ 425
193	M33.15-r.1	2	$ 110
194	M33.17-r.1	4	$ 80
195	M33.17-r.5	7	$ 650
196	M33.27-r.4	6	$ 165
197	M33.1-4.4	2	$ 70
198	M31.2-r.3	1	$ 500

199	M31.1-gg.1	3	$ 900
200	M30-hh.2	2	$ 325
201	M44-Z.10	7	$ 235
202	M44-W.4	3	$ 250
203	M44-W.5	7	$ 170
204	M33.26-W.5	7	$ 235
205	M33.26-W.3	7	$ 200
206	M33.44-W.3	7	$ 800
207	M33.25-W.3	7	$ 500
208	M33.12-W.3	7	$ 340
209	M33.3-W.1	4	$ 70
210	M33.45-W2	7	$ 375
211	M33.34-W2	6	$ 275
212	M33.10-W-6	8(o)	$ 475
213	M33.19-q	7	$ 225
214	M33.43-q	6	$ 140
215	M33.4-q	6	$ 185
216	M33.6-KK	3	$ 170
217	M33.37-Z.9	4	$ 450
218	M33.43-hh.2	6	$ 300
219	M.ee.23-hh.2	7	$ 275
220	M33.13-hh.2	7	$ 325
221	M33.4-Z.2	6	$ 210
222	M33.42-Z.2	7	$ 210
223	M33.19-Z.2	5	$ 200
224	M33.40-Z.2	7	$ 825
225	M33.23-Z.4	3	$ 75
226	M33.2-Z.17	6	$ 140
227	M33.13-Z.1	7	$ 350
228	M33.19-Z.1	1	$ 85
229	M33.38-Z.1	5	$ 72
230	M33.40-Z.1	7	$ 275
231	M33.12-Z.21	7	$ 235
232	M33.2-Z.21	7	$ 300
233	M33.2-Z.22	7	$ 150
234	M33.13-Z.6	6	$ 300
235	M33.38-Z.6	6	$ 120
236	M33.35-Z.9	8(p)	$ 275
237	M33.20-Z.9	6	$ 300
239	M33.20-Z.9	6	$ 400
240	M33.20-Z.11	8(q)	$ 125
241	M33.34-Z.11	6	$ 300

242	M33.33-Z.3	6	$ 335
243	M33.34-Z.3	6	$ 300
244	M33.12-Z.24	7	$ 800
245	M33.12-Z.16	3	$ 600
246	M33.18-Z.24	8(r)	$ 550
247	M33.25-Z.24	7	$ 210
248	M33.25-Z.10	6	$ 350
249	M33.24-Z.10	8(s)	$ 300
250	M33.28-Z.16	3	$ 275
251	M33.28-Z.11	3	$ 500
252	M33.10-Z.8	6	$ 425
253	M33.19-Z.4	8(t)	$ 325
254	M33.10-Z.7	6	$ 285
255	M33.38-Z.23	6	$ 425
256	M33.48-Z.25	8(u)	$ 900
257	M33.29-Z.25	8(v)	$ 250
258	M33.29-Z.7	7	$ 195
259	M33.13-Z.7	6	$ 315
260	M33.39-Z.20	7	$ 245
261	M33.39-Z.13	8(w)	$ 300
262	M33.8-Z.13	6	$ 460
263	M33.8-Z.19	6	$ 600
264	M33.21-Z.13	7	$ 385
265	M33.1-Z.19	6	$ 460
266	M33.1-Z.13	5	$ 260
267	M33.32-Z.13	1	$ 375
268	M33.2-Z.12	1	$ 425
269	M33.2-Z.5	1	$ 125
270	M32.11-Z.18	5	$ 190
271	M33.16-Z.15	2	$ 100
272	M33.14-Z.14	4	$ 425
273	M.30-X.1	5	$ 85
274	M32.4-Z.3		$ 325
275	M43.1-Y	1	$ 150
276	M43.2-X.4	7	$ 250
277	M32.3-X.4	1	$ 110
278	M32.2-X.4	7	$ 300
279	M32.2-X.2	2	$ 200
280	M32.2-X.1	1	$ 185
281	M32.7-X.1	6	$ 210
282	M32.1-X.3	5	$ 180
283	M32.4-X.5	6	$ 300

284	M32.6-X.6	6	$ 250
285	M32.5-aa	4	$ 90
286	M32.8-aa	7	$ 160

THE 1788 VARIETIES

287	M1-I	7	$2200
288	M.3-B.1	6	$ 300
289	M.3-B.2	7	$1500
290	M.5-B.2	6	$ 600
291	M.4.1-K	6	$ 375
292	M4.1-B.1	6	$ 225
293	M4.2-R	7	$ 300
294	M.6-H	7	$ 375
295	M.2-D	1	$ 575
296	M.13-A.1	6	$ 275
297	M.11-G	3	$ 210
298	M.10-C	7	$ 300
299	M.12.2-C	4	$ 190
300	M.12.2-E	4	$ 230
301	M.12.1-F.1	4	$ 800
302	M.12.1-E	4	$ 135
303	M.9-E	6	$ 200
304	M.7-E	6	$ 275
305	M.7-F.2	8(x)	$ 450
306	M.7-K	7	$ 225
307	M.8-K	7	$ 200
308	M.14-L.2	6	$ 135
309	M.14.2-A.2	6	$ 275
310	M.15.1-L.1	5	$ 300
311	M.15.2-P	5	$ 190
312	M.16.1-D	3	$ 175
313	M.16.1-H	3	$ 100
314	M.16.2-O	6	$ 185
316	M.16.3-N	3	$ 160
318	M.16.4-A.2	8(y)	$ 200
319	M.16.4-L.2	6	$ 125
319A	M.16.4-L.2	6	$1500(z)
320	M.16.5-H	6	$ 125
321	M16.6-H	7	$ 185
322	M16.7-P	7	$ 150
323	M.17-Q	6	$ 250
324	M.4.1-F.4	1	$ 35

325	M.6.2-F.1	4	$ 300
326	M.7.1-D	7	$ 250
327	M1.-A	6	$ 150
328	M2.1-A	3	$ 200
329	M.3-D.1	6	$ 175
331	M4.5-G	2	$ 375
333	M5.11-R	7	$ 175
334	M.6-k	6	$ 250
335	M.1.3-L	7	$ 150
339	M.52-G.1	7	$ 160
340	M.50-F	7	$ 250
341	M.9-R	7	$ 500
343	M.12-Q	6	$ 300
346	M.15-S	7	$ 300
347	M.41-ii	4	$ 225
351	M.39.1-H.1	6	$ 245
354	M.37.8-LL	5	$ 500
357	M.33.7-r.2	1	$ 350
358	M.33.17-gg.2	?	$ 750
364	M.33.6-kk	?	$ 150
367	M.33.10-Z.7	6	$ 125
368	M.33.21-Z.13	7	$ 300
371	M33.2-Z.5	1	$ 70
372	M43.1-Y	?	$ 95
377	M.3-B.1	6	$ 140
378	M.3-B.1	6	$ 45
379	M.5-B.2	7	$ 120
380	M.4.1-K	6	$ 150
381	M.4.1-B.1	7	$ 225
382	M.4.2-R	7	$ 75
383	M.6-H	7	$ 100
387	M.10-C	7	$ 40
392	M.15.1-L.1	6	$ 95
394	M16.1-H	3	$ 100

(a)	Not in Miller or Ryder
(b)	Unlisted Muling
(c)	Called 5.12-L by Miller
(d)	Unpublished Unique Muling
(e)	Unique
(f)	Not in Miller
(g)	Unique

(h)	Not in Miller
(i)	Not in Miller
(j)	Possibly unique
(k)	Not in Miller
(l)	Possibly unique
(m)	Not in Miller
(n)	Unique
(o)	Semi-unique
(p)	Semi-unique
(q)	Semi-unique
(r)	Semi-unique
(s)	Unique, unpublished
(t)	Unique
(u)	Unique, unlisted
(v)	Semi-unique, unlisted
(w)	Semi-unique, unlisted
(x)	Only 4 known
(y)	Unlisted Mule
(z)	Choice uncirculated

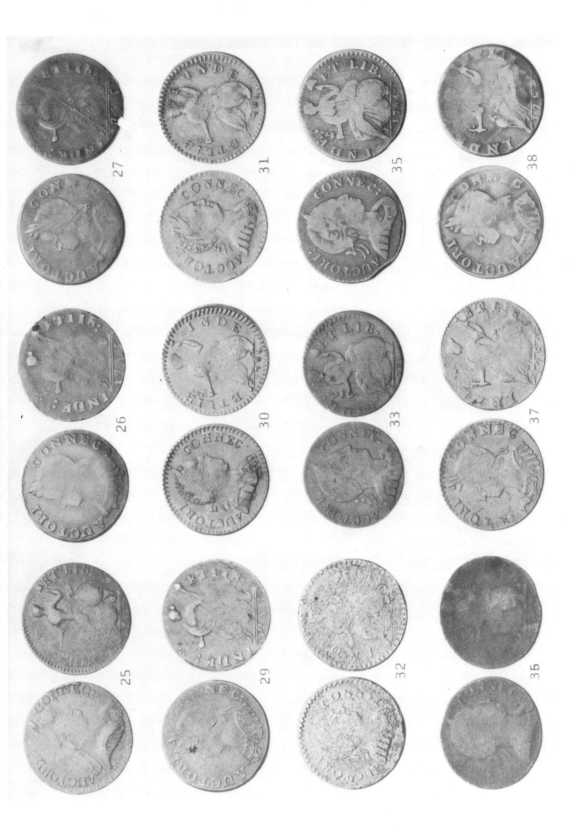

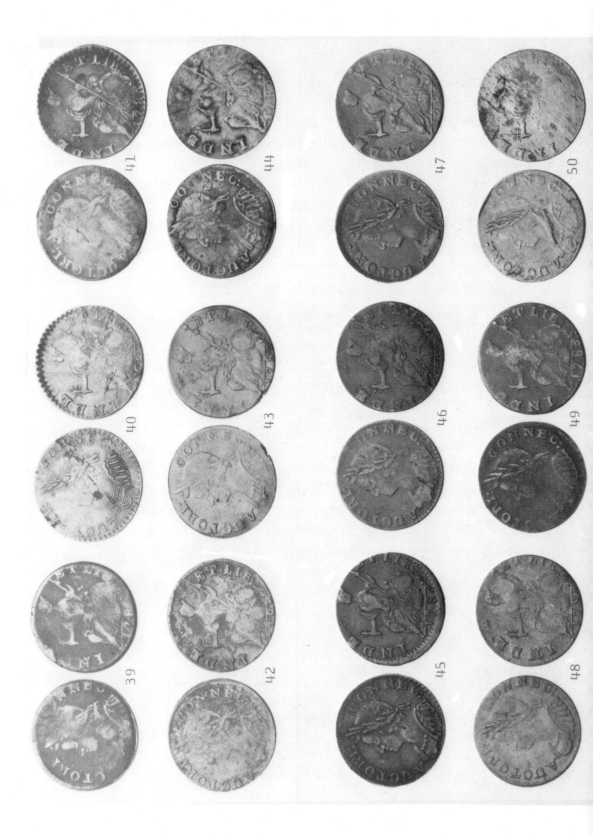

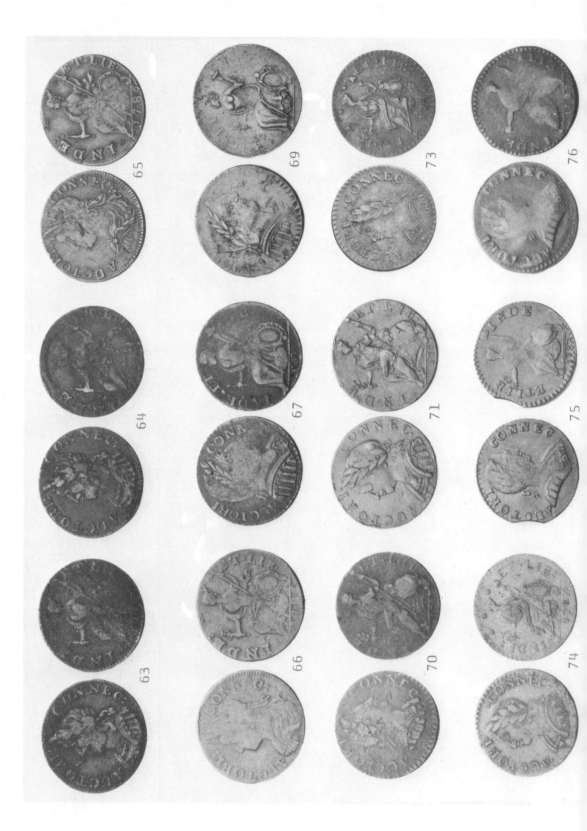

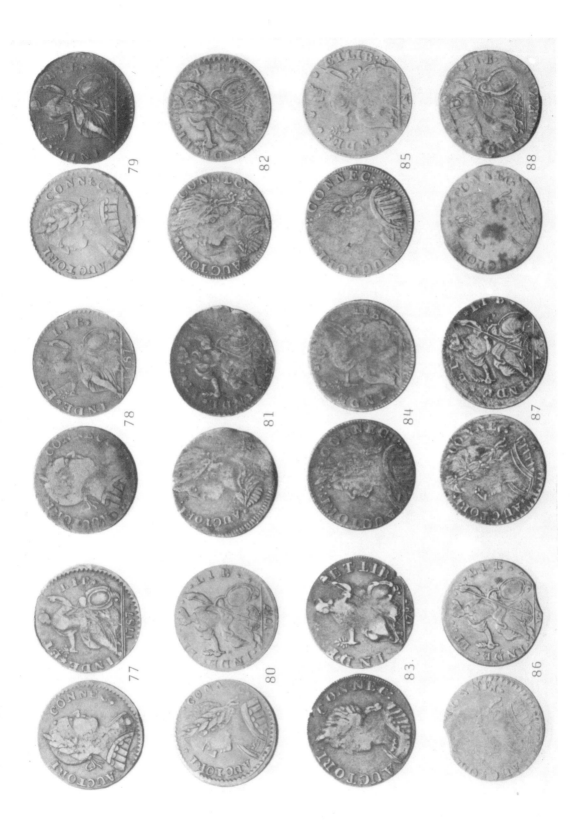

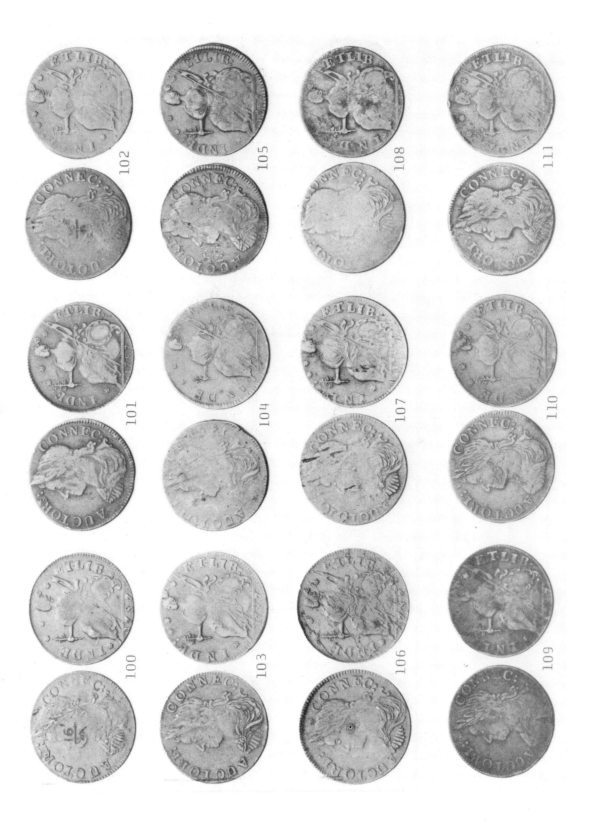

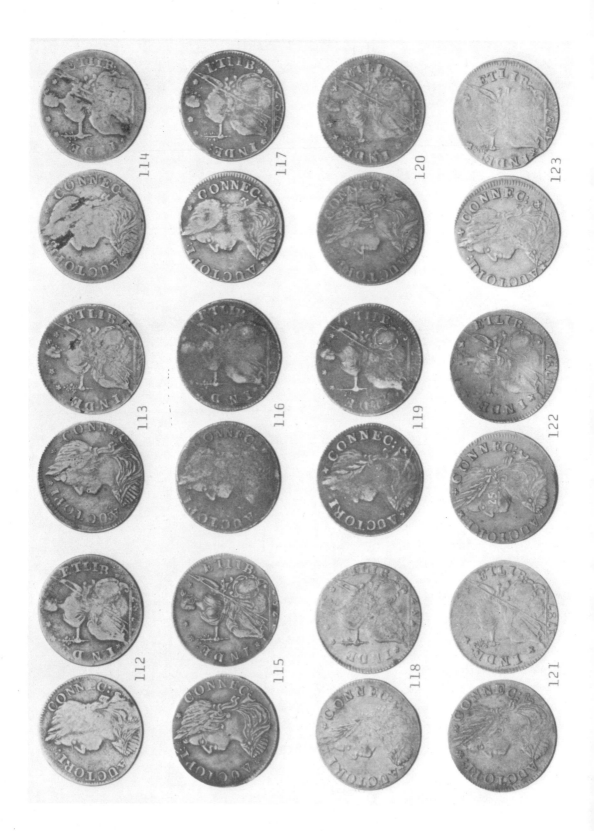

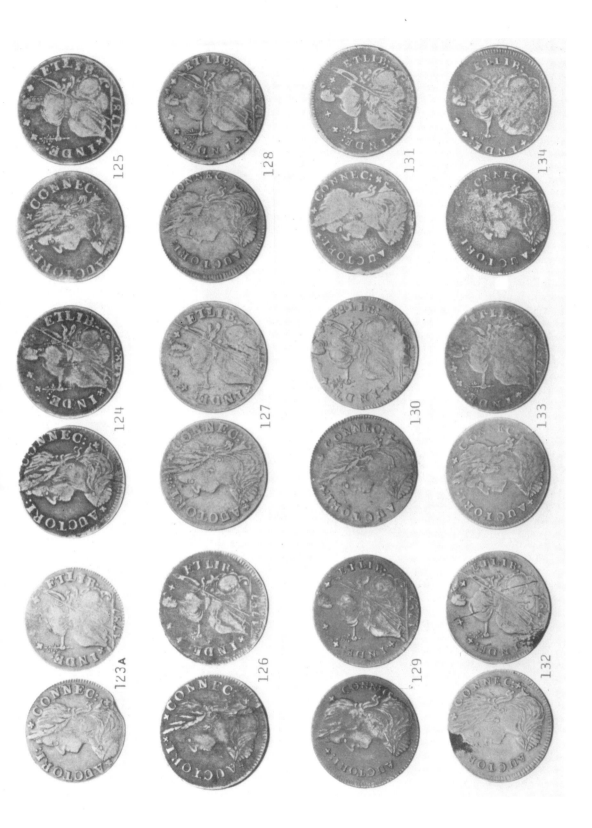

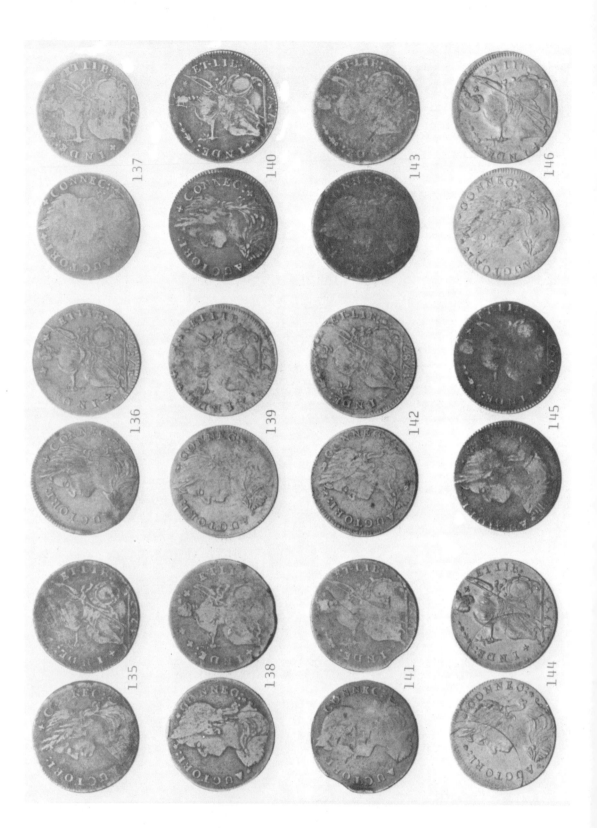

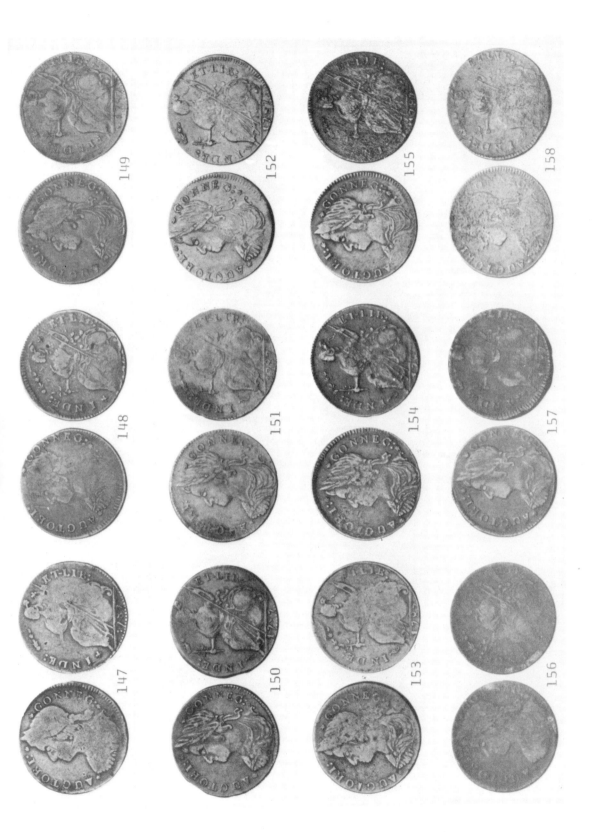

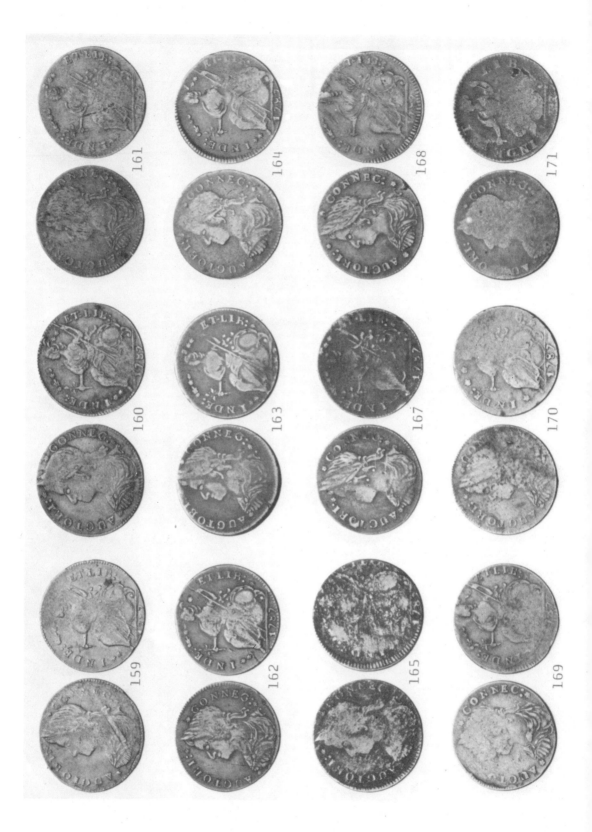

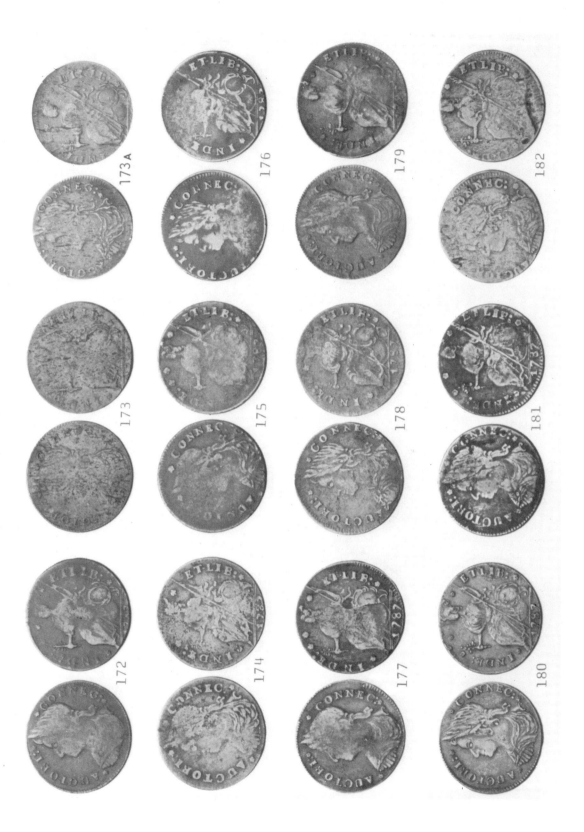

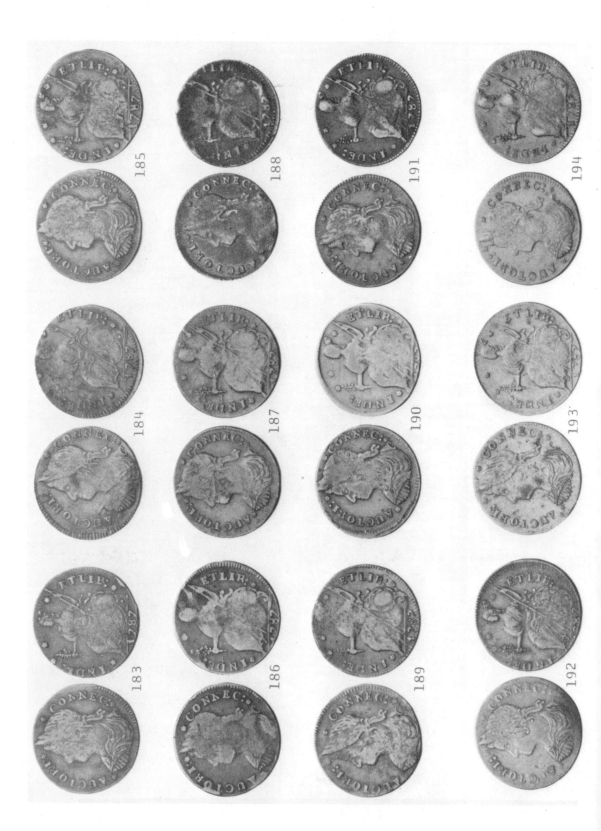

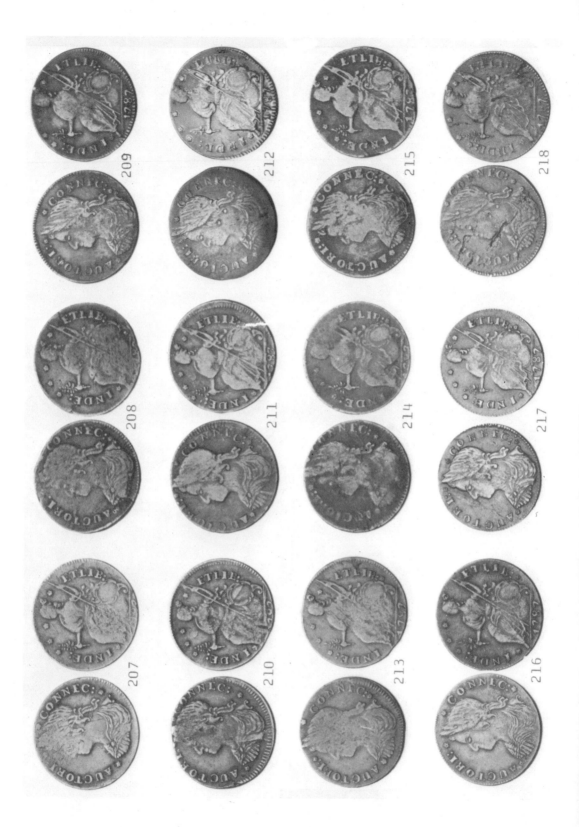

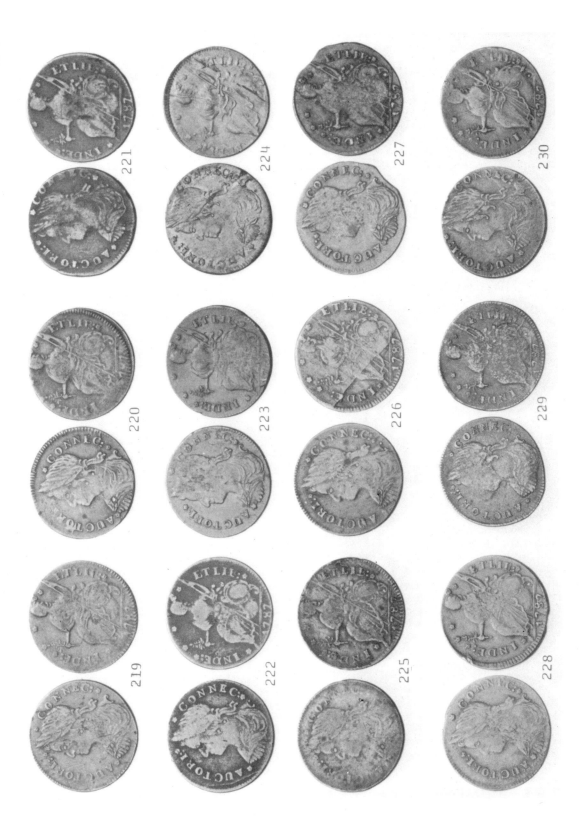

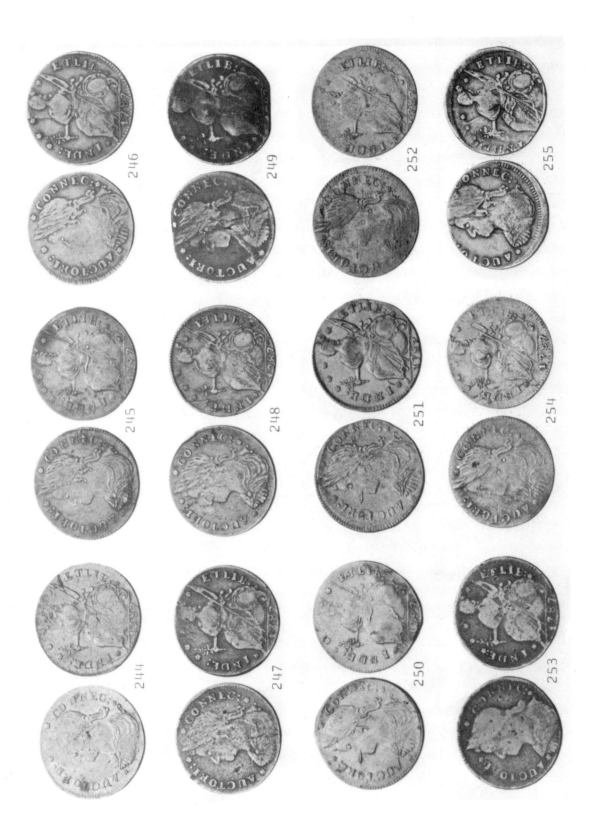

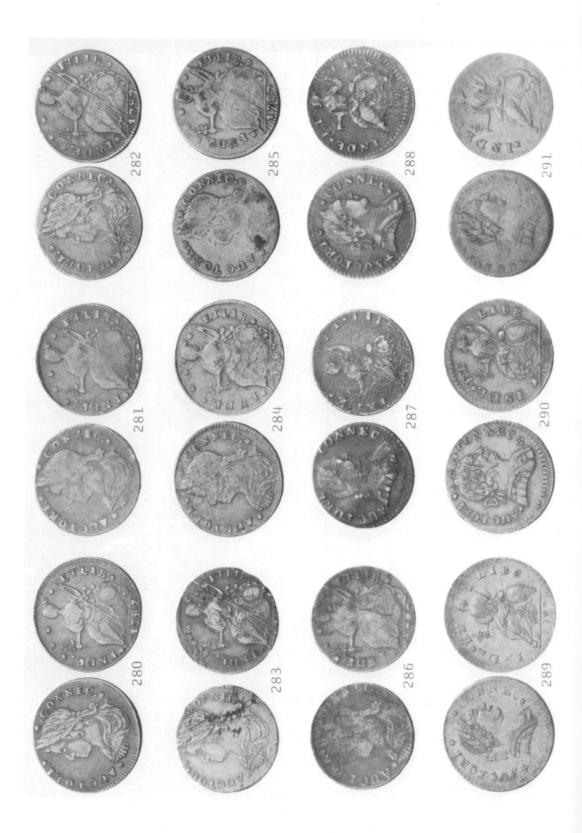

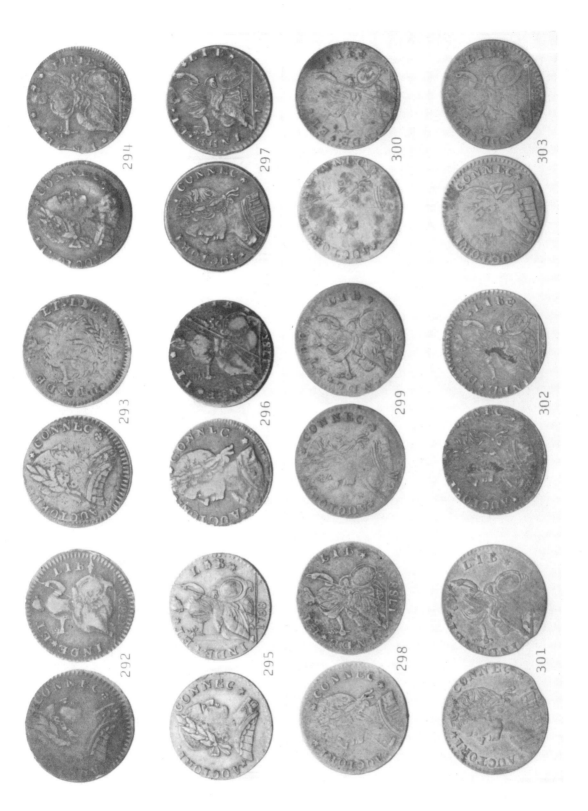

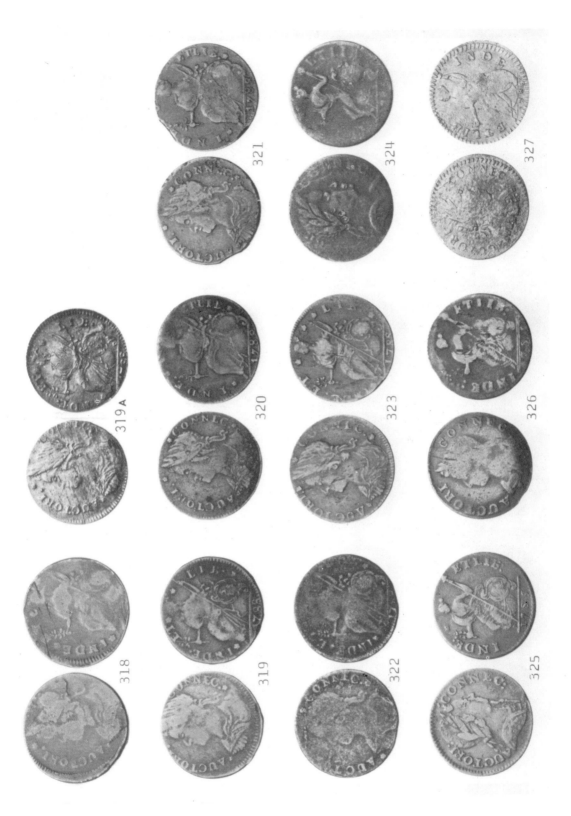

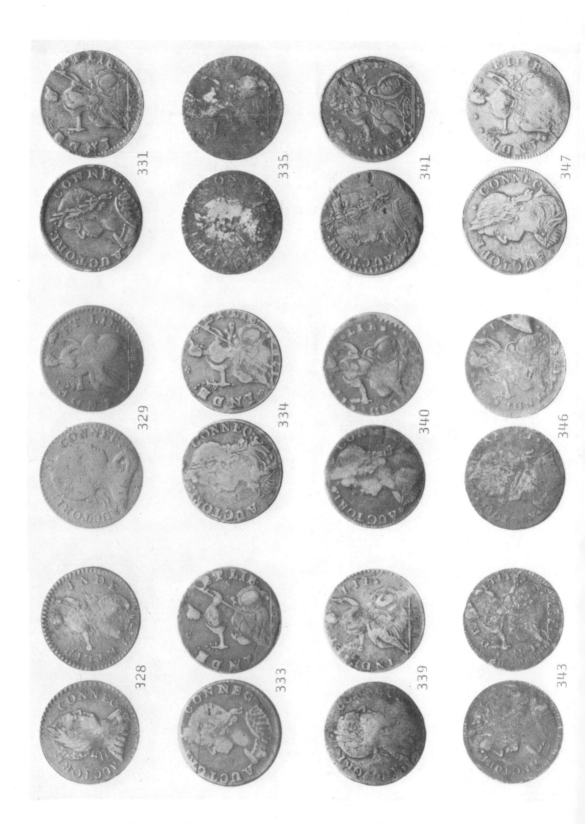

SELECTED READING AND BIBLIOGRAPHY
ON THE COLONIAL COINAGE OF THE U.S.

Atkins, James: "Tradesmans Tokens of the Eighteenth Century" 1892.

Baker, William S.: "Medallic Portraits of Washington", 1885.

Benton, William: "The Annals of America", 1968.

Betts, C. Wyllys: "American Colonial History", 1894.

Betts, C. Wyllys: "Counterfeit Halfpence Current in the American Colonies", American Numismatic & Archaeological Society, April 1886.

Breen, Walter: "The United States Patterns of 1792", The Coin Collector's Journal, March–April 1954.

Breen, Walter: "Encyclopedia of United States and Colonial Proof Coins (1722–1977), 1977.

Breton, P.N.: "Popular Illustrated Guide to Canadian Coins", 1894.

Brown, Vernon L.: "The Brasher Doubloon", The Numismatist, June, 1964.

Crosby, Sylvester S.: "The Early Coins of America", Boston 1875 Reprinted 1945, 1965, 1974.

Dickeson, M.W.: "American Numismatic Manual", 1859 Philadelphia.

Douglas, Damon G.: "British-American Colonial Coins", The Numismatist, April 1948.

Durst, Sanford J.: Comprehensive Guide to American Colonial Coinage, 1976.

Fuld, George and Melvin: "The Talbot, Allum, and Lee Cents", The Numismatic Scrapbook reprint, September, 1956.

Guttag Brothers: "Cents of New Jersey", 1927.

Hancock, Virgil and Spanbauer, Larry: Standard Catalog of United States Altered and Counterfeit Coins, 1979.

Hawkins, R.N.P.: "Dictionary of Birmingham Makers of Metallic Tickets, Checks, and Counters", Seaby's Coin and Medal Bulletin, May, 1960.

Hawley, Cyril H.: "Auctori Connec and the Fugio's", Auctori Connec and Other Emissions, 1959.

Hickcox, John H.: "Historical Account of American Coinage", 1858.

Higgens, Frank C.: "The Washington Cents", Monthly Numismatic Circular, Spink and Sons, April 1902.

J.F.J.: "The North American Token–1781", The Numismatist, June, 1937.

Kenney, Richard D.: "Struck Copies of Early American Coins", 1952.

Kenney, Richard D.: "Early American Medalists and Die Sinkers", Coin Collector's Journal, January–February, 1954.

Kurth, Howard H.: "The Albany Church Pennies", Numismatic Scrapbook, April, 1944.

Maris, Edward.: "A Historical Sketch of the Coins of New Jersey", Philadelphia 1881. (Reprinted 1925)

Mehl, B. Max: "The Spanish Doubloon Coined by Brasher", James Ten Eyck Sale, May, 1922.

Miller, Henry C. & Ryder, H.: "The State Coinage of Connecticut", American Journal of Numismatics, 1920.

Moore, Richard D.: "The Higley Coppers, 1737–1739:, Auctori Connec and Other Emissions, 1959.

Morin, Victor: "Castorland", The Numismatist, October, 1942.

Nelson, Philip: "The Coinage of Ireland in Copper, Tin, and Pewter", 1905.

Nelson, Philip: "The Coinage of William Wood, 1722–1733", London 1903. (Reprinted 1959)

Newman, Eric O.: "A Recently Discovered Coin Solves a Vermont Numismatic Enigma", Centennial Publication of the American Numismatic Society, 1958.

Newman, Eric P.: "Coinage for Colonial Virginia", American Numismatic Society, 1956.

Newman, Eric P.: "Additions to Coinage for Colonial Virginia", Museum notes X, American Numismatic Society, 1962.

Newman, Eric P.: "First Documentary Evidence on the American Colonial Pewter, 1/24th Real", The Numismatist, July, 1955.

Newman, Eric P.: "The 1775 Continental Currency Coinage", Coin Collectors Journal, July–August, 1952.

Newman, Eric P.: "Varieties of the Fugio Cent", Coin Collectors Journal July–August, 1952.

Newman, Eric P.: "The Secret of the Good Samaritan Shilling", New York, 1959.

Newman, Eric P. and Doty, Richard, "Studies on Money in Early America", 1978.

Noe, Sydney P.: "Oak Tree Coinage of Massachusetts", American Numismatic Society, 1947.

Noe, Sydney P.: "Pine Tree Coinage of Massachusetts", American Numismatic Society, 1952.

Noe, Sydney P.: "New England and Willow Tree Coinage of Massachusetts", American Numismatic Society, 1943.

Peck, C. Wilson: "British Copper, Tin and Bronze Coins in the British Museum, 1558–1958", 1960.

Perlitz, William F.: "John Chalmers, Issue of the Annapolis Coinage", The Numismatist, November, 1948.

Peterson, Haven: "Background of American Coinage", The Numismatist, 1953.

Pine Tree Auctions, Inc., Catalog of February 15, 1975 Sale.

Raymond, Wayte: "Standard Catalog of United State Coins", 1957.

Richardson, John M.: "The Copper Coins of Vermont", The Numismatist, 1947.

Ryder, Hillyer: "Copper Coins of Massachusetts", 1920.

Ryder, Hillyer: "Coinage of Vermont", 1920.

Steigerwald, Charles: "Illustrated History of United States and Colonial Coins".

Taxay, Don: "Catalog and Encyclopedia of U.S. Coins", 1976.

"The American Numismatic Society Exhibition of United States and Colonial Coins Catalog", 1914.

Vlack, Robert A.: "Early American Coins", 1965.

Wurtzbach, Carl: "Massachusetts Colonial Silver Money", 1937.

Yeoman, R.S.: "A Guide Book of United States Coins", published annually.

DURST PUBLICATIONS
(Includes Forthcoming Titles)

FOREIGN

Cresswell, O.D., CHINESE CASH $8.00
Davis, W. J., NINETEENTH CENTURY TOKEN COINAGE $35.00
Durst, S. J., CONTEMPORARY WORLD GOLD COINS $10.00
Frey, A. & Cervin, D., DATED COINAGE OF EUROPE PRIOR TO 1501 $25.00
Hawkins, E., SILVER COINS OF ENGLAND $45.00
Kann, E., CURRENCIES OF CHINA $39.50
Kann, E., ILLUSTRATED CATALOG OF CHINESE COINS $50.00
Katz, V., A THOUSAND YEARS OF BOHEMIAN COINAGE 929–1929 $10.00
Kenyon, L., THE GOLD COINS OF ENGLAND $30.00
Kraus, D. R., SWISS SHOOTING TALERS & MEDALS $10.00
Pradeau, A., NUMISMATIC HISTORY OF MEXICO $25.00
Sadow, J. & Sarro, T., COINS & MEDALS OF THE VATICAN $13.00
Scholten, C., COINS OF THE DUTCH OVERSEAS TERRITORIES $35.00
Wang, Y., EARLY CHINESE COINAGE $35.00

ANCIENT

Baldwin, A., SYMBOLISM ON GREEK COINS $16.50
Baldwin, A., FACING HEADS ON ANCIENT GREEK COINS $7.50
Bellinger, A., ESSAYS ON THE COINAGE OF ALEXANDER THE GREAT $30.00
Bellinger, A., TROY THE COINS $39.50
Bellinger, A., SYRIAN TETRADRACHMS $26.00
Gardner, P., SAMOS AND SAMIAN COINS $30.00
Grant, M., ANCIENT HISTORY ATLAS $10.00
Head, B., COINAGE OF LYDIA AND PERSIA $30.00
Icard, S., DICTIONARY OF GREEK COIN INSCRIPTIONS $42.50
Klawans, Z. OUTLINE OF ANCIENT GREEK COINS $10.00
Newell, E. T., STANDARD PTOLEMAIC SILVER $6.00
Rogers, E., HANDY GUIDE TO JEWISH COINS $15.00
Starr, C., ATHENIAN COINAGE $20.00
Sutherland, H., COINAGE OF THE ROMAN IMPERIAL POLICY $22.50
Sydnham, E., COINAGE OF THE ROMAN REPUBLIC $27.50

UNITED STATES

Adams, E., ADAM'S OFFICIAL PREMIUM LIST OF UNITED STATES PRIVATE & TERRITORIAL GOLD COINS $10.00
Adams, E., UNITED STATES STORE CARDS $12.00
Browning, A. W., EARLY QUARTER DOLLARS $15.00
Durst, S. J., EARLY AMERICAN COPPERS ANTHOLOGY $39.50
Durst, S. J., COMPREHENSIVE GUIDE TO AMERICAN COLONIAL COINAGE $18.00
Evans, G., HISTORY OF THE U.S. MINT & COINAGE $15.00
Government, U.S., HISTORY OF THE BUREAU OF ENGRAVING & PRINTING $25.00
Knox, J. J., UNITED STATES NOTES $22.50
Low, L. H., HARD TIMES TOKENS $16.00
Maris, E., COINS OF NEW JERSEY $15.00
Miller, H. C., STATE COINAGE OF CONNECTICUT $15.00
Nelson, P., COINAGE OF WILLIAM WOOD $6.00
Newman, E. P., COINS OF COLONIAL VIRGINIA $15.00
Newman, E. P., & Bressett, K., FANTASTIC 1804 DOLLAR $15.00
Ryder, H., COLONIAL COINS OF VERMONT $10.00
Ryder, H., COPPER COINS OF MASSACHUSETTS $5.00
Schuckers, J., FINANCES & PAPER MONEY OF THE REVOLUTIONARY WAR $15.00
Spanbauer, L. & Hancock, V., STANDARD CATALOG OF U.S. COUNTERFEIT COINS $30.00
   Luxury edition, numbered 1–1000 $37.50
Taxay, D., U.S. MINT & COINAGE $25.00
Valentine, FRACTIONAL CURRENCY OF THE U.S. $10.00

GENERAL

Durst, S. J., COLLECTOR/INVESTOR GUIDEBOOK $15.00
Durst, S. J. & L., WORLD SILVER COINS VALUE GUIDE, softcover $9.00
   Hardcover $12.00
Durst, S. J. & L., WORLD GOLD COINS VALUE GUIDE, softcover $9.00
   Hardcover $12.00
Durst, L. S., UNITED STATES NUMISMATIC AUCTION CATALOGS: A BIBLIOGRAPHY $35.00
Kosoff, A., ABE KOSOFF REMEMBERS . . . , softcover $19.50
   Hardcovered, Numbered 1–500 $30.00
   Leatherbound, Numbered 1–100 $125.00
Lawrence, R. H., MEDALS OF GIOVANNI CAVINO, THE PADUAN $5.00
Levine, E., THE GOLDEN KEY (An investment analysis of all forms of gold) $35.00
Low, L. H., OBSERVATIONS ON THE PRACTICE OF COUNTERFEITING COINS & MEDALS $2.00
Reed, F. M., ODD & CURIOUS, SOFTCOVER, Volume I $7.00
   Hardcover, Volume I $12.50
   Volume II Forthcoming at same prices
Welter, G. & Schulman, H., CLEANING & PRESERVATION OF COINS & MEDALS $12.00

PHILATELICS

Dalson, T., Lewes, T. & Pemberton, E., EARLY FORGED STAMPS DETECTOR, Softcovered $10.00
   Hardcovered $16.00
Woodward, P. H., SECRET SERVICE OF THE U.S. POST OFFICE $35.00

SANFORD J. DURST
170 EAST 61st STREET, NEW YORK, NEW YORK 10021, 212 593-3514